Humane and practical, Fran Newman tak[es us into the real] classroom, and shows us real ways to co[p] enable true learning.

From the foreword [

. . . helps redefine the art of listening to include ....g helping.

Joyce Nesker Simmons
Education Columnist, Toronto Sun

An outstanding description of the "troubled world" our children are coping with in their daily lives . . . a much needed support document for the human service providers working in the school system.

Lena White
Native Human Services Program, Laurentian University

This wise, bracing and practical book will encourage caring adults to explore their untapped potential to help kids in need.

Rona Maynard
columnist and contributing editor to Pathways

. . . covers many very sensitive, controversial and often ignored issues that can occur in the world of a child with medical problems.

Lynda Hoffman
Director of Education, Epilepsy Ontario

. . . a valuable resource for teachers and others who come in contact with troubled children.

Heather Sproule
Executive Director, Canadian Children's Foundation

A much needed book which addresses many of the questions which teachers, in particular, address to me when I conduct workshops on self-esteem, humor and health, AIDS and coping with disability.

Dr. Arlette Lefebvre
Psychiatrist, The Hospital for Sick Children, Toronto

It is such a pleasure to read a book that is so child-centered.

Kathy Lynn
Parenting Today

Children
in
Crisis

• • •

SUPPORT FOR TEACHERS
AND PARENTS

Fran Newman

foreword by
Michele Landsberg

Scholastic Canada Ltd.

To Bill Bridge, former principal, mentor and friend; to Mary Labatt, editor of the Federation of Women Teachers of Ontario Newsletter, who has been so supportive; to the many teachers who have attended my workshops and shown their warm hearts in their caring and concern; and especially to the children, who continue to teach me.

I also want to thank all those caring people who supported me, directly or indirectly, through my own pain and growth to independence: Leo Buscaglia, Catherine Marshall, Paul Tournier, Scott Peck, Alice Miller, John Bradshaw, John Powell, William Purkey, Barbara Coloroso, Robin Norwood, Louise Hay, Shakti Gawain, Susan Jeffers, Virginia Satir, June Callwood, Merle Shain, Colette Dowling, and so many more.

The hurting children described in this book are real children. Some, I have taught myself; some, other teachers have told me about. In a few cases, I've changed details to protect the identity of families whose circumstances were never made public.

FN

Canadian Cataloguing in Publication Data

Newman, Fran, 1937—
   Children in crisis

Includes bibliographical references.
ISBN 0-590-73088-6

1. Children - Counseling of. 2. Child mental health. I. Title.

HV713.N49 1993   362.7   C92-095738-2

CONTENTS

Foreword

An ancient Jewish proverb says: "Without butter, there is no learning." Frightened, angry, lonely or hungry children do not learn; children who think themselves stupid or inadequate do not bloom intellectually.

Unfortunately, many children today come to school hungry, confused, at sea in the foreign sounds of English, or cut loose and drifting from the affectionate family support we used to take for granted. At the same time, many concerted and powerful voices boom out a demand for more tests, more "standards," more authority, more control. Control versus care — an almost classic case of patriarchal values against nurturing principles.

We live in an era of conservative values in almost every aspect of life, and many Canadians accept the currents of the time as though they were simple common sense and recognized wisdom. And so we have an intense and disquieting irony. Just when economic policies have produced a tidal wave of deprivation, the victims of those policies unquestioningly accept outdated educational views as the solution to our schooling problems.

Many parents, anxious about their children's future in a threatening economic climate, believe the myth that there was a "golden era" of education when everyone learned the basics, and that we can go back to that never-never land by sheer force of will.

The truth is that as late as the 1950s the average Canadian never finished high school, and only a tiny handful of the elite went on to university. The vast majority were expected to proceed directly to menial or blue-collar jobs, many of which no longer exist. Any child who did not fit the homogenous, narrow "norm" — any child who learned at a different pace, spoke another language, came from a different culture — was simply dumped or left to sink or swim.

The very parents whose children would suffer most from a return to those narrow days are now the most eager to turn back the clock. They demand the return of the Three R's, standardized tests, rigid drills and rote work. They maintain the desperate belief that such methods will somehow ensure their children's successful future employment.

These same people echo the conservative pundits, many of whom seem quite out of touch with the day-to-day responsibilities of nurturing and educating children. They reject talk of "self-esteem," react against literature-based and whole language teaching, and question the value and wisdom of "child-centered" education.

The longing for simple solutions, unfortunately, leads inevitably to inadequate answers. Our schools are attempting to educate a huge diversity of children in a complex and demanding world. And parents have far higher expectations of achievement than ever prevailed in those dim Three R's days when curiosity, higher-level thinking and intellectual adventure were punished rather than rewarded.

In the midst of all this turmoil, classroom teachers must confront the clamoring human reality of individual children, including those whose hearts are broken or whose bodies are bruised.

Fran Newman, in this earthy and experience-based book, addresses the question of those individual children and the teachers who must help them learn. She does not issue prescriptions for curriculum reform. Instead, she puts into words what good teachers and caring parents know: Attention must be paid. Human needs must be met. The mind is not separate from the body. Emotional traumas are not checked at the classroom door.

Teachers are not therapists, but our society has dropped into their laps the overwhelming task of educating children to an ever-higher "standard" of achievement, while living standards plummet and families break apart under the strain.

Children in Crisis warmly encompasses the human reality of all the children who may be ignored or dismissed in the current rush to implement a conservative ethos. It deals with "bottom-up" strategies rather than "top-down" authoritarian mechanisms.

I think parents and teachers alike will respond with exhilaration and hope to Fran Newman's optimistic spirit as she plunges into the fray. Humane and practical, she takes us into real classrooms and shows us real ways to cope, to thrive and to enable true learning.

Michele Landsberg

INTRODUCTION

This is primarily a book for teachers. But it is also for other professionals working with children and for parents. I am both a parent and a teacher. The main focus of my life has been children — my own, their friends, my students.

Over the last decade, part of my teaching time has focused on counseling children. Of course, all teachers are counselors at times, but many are hesitant and unsure. As I learned and gained confidence, I shared my experiences with others. Eventually I was asked by the Federation of Women Teachers of Ontario (FWTO) to provide workshops for my colleagues. At the same time, I wrote a series of articles in the *FWTO Newsletter*. Responses to those workshops and articles made clear the need for a broader, more comprehensive support tool for people dealing with hurting children. This book is the result.

The more I learned, the more the traditional distinctions between home and school began to blur for me. This book is about pain in the lives of people — any people, all people. Thinking about the pain some of my students were suffering made me reflect on the painful memories of my own childhood. Watching them trying to cope with loss through separation and divorce, serious illness, or death made me experience again the pain of being left to parent one son and four daughters on my own. Researching the coping topics of the book reminded me that I had not been a perfect parent for my own family. Like every parent of grown children, I would like to turn back the clock for parts of my parenting.

So I hope that many parents will read this book. I hope that it will help some to remember or acknowledge their own pain and to recognize the hurt their children may be experiencing. And I hope that, through it, they will come to understand how different education is now from when they went to school.

Teaching is changing. Students are changing. Curriculum is changing. Some of those changes are marvelous. New literature-based and natural-learning approaches focus on the needs of children as traditional schooling could not. New guidance programs, particularly in drug and sex education, are full of promise. But now, more than ever before, the teaching profession is under stress.

In October, 1989, the widely read Canadian magazine, *Chatelaine*, ran some articles on the crisis in teaching. It described teachers as "frontline social workers" trying to educate students who are affected by family trauma and breakdown, by poverty, and by the false promises of drugs and promiscuity. Today's society not only asks teachers to teach children to read, to write, and to do arithmetic, it also asks them to provide morals and values, and to be positive role models. Officially, we are trained to teach the academic curriculum, but we have only our instincts and experience as human beings for most of the "hidden curriculum."

In March, 1990, the *Toronto Star*, Canada's largest newspaper, ran a front-page story with the headline: "Out-of-control kids put schools in crisis." The story echoed *Chatelaine*, pointing to an increase in home violence that has led to increased violence in schools. Whatever the reasons, more and more children seem to lack the basic social know-how we used to take for granted, and teachers struggle to teach students who seem unreachable and unteachable. The *Star's* conclusion: teachers have not been trained to help kids deal with such sweeping trauma!

Think about a typical classroom. Of 25 students, how many

- are being physically and/or emotionally abused?
- were or are being sexually abused?
- will become seriously ill?
- will experience the death of someone they care about?
- come from a separated, divorced, or blended family?
- live in an alcoholic home?
- have been limited or put down because of their color or sex?

Each school and each classroom has its own profile, but my own experiences and research offer something like the following.

- One out of two is physically abused, if you include as abuse all corporal punishment even slightly over judicial and fair limits.
- One in four girls, one in ten boys has been or is being sexually assaulted.
- One may become seriously ill during the year or experience serious illness in the family.
- Two or three will see a grandparent or a favorite relative or family friend die.
- Approximately half will come from living situations where the biological parents are not together.

It is all very immediate and personal for me. When I walk into my classroom on any given morning, I know that many of those children are hurting inside. However, few of us were trained to recognize the signals children give us in their behavior, their play, their writing, their art, their demeanor.

The signals are particularly apparent in their classroom and school behavior. All teachers have a few students they wish were someone else's responsibility: the obnoxious ones, the troublemakers, the whiners, the truants. Teachers often feel lost and helpless when trying to deal with these children. I know a grade four teacher who tries hard not to be sick because no supply teacher will take her class. Sometimes teachers think to themselves: get rid of all the troublemakers and let me teach!

The important message of this book is that *every single one of those children is hurting*. They act the way they do because they have so little defense against a world that, for them, has not been a kind place.

Almost every child comes into the world with an amazing "Hey, world, here I am!" face. The fortunate ones have stable, confident parents who raise them in an atmosphere of acceptance and support for the growing up they have to do. Their behavior at school tends to mirror that stability — they make teaching a pleasure. The unfortunate ones live in emotionally and physically unstable situations almost from birth. Their behavior, too, mirrors what they have learned — sometimes they challenge their teachers' humanity.

How do teachers recognize the children who bring serious problems to school, especially when the children themselves often do not recognize their own problems? The irony is that children from troubled homes often believe that all families are like theirs. How can teachers reach and support those children on top of their "real" job — to teach the curriculum?

In fact, notions of curriculum are also changing. Prominent researchers like Indiana University's Jerome Harste are beginning to say that children are the curriculum. From my own experience I would add, never more than when they are hurting. For many children, school is the safest place in their world; it is the place where adults set out deliberately to know and care about them, work with them, show them compassion, and demonstrate responsibility. Teachers may not be able to change the circumstances these children face outside the school building, but they can help to ensure that the time they spend in school is safe and good.

To do that, teachers also need help.

• • • • •

A teacher reads in a student's journal that his father came home drunk again last night. The boy is becoming afraid — what can he do?

• • • • •

A teacher comes to school in the morning and the principal tells him that the parent of one of his students was killed the night before.

• • • • •

A teacher discovers that one of the girls in her grade eight class is pregnant.

• • • • •

A girl's mother ran off with another man some time ago. Today is the mother's birthday and the student grieves openly in class all day.

• • • • •

A student from an abusive home situation has a raging temper tantrum when the teacher makes her sit in her own seat.

• • • • •

I am a good teacher, but I am not always sure what to do in circumstances like these. I used to deal with such cases on instinct alone, using the expertise I had gained as a parent. I care, and have always cared about children. For many years I have shared the joys, frustrations, fights, anger, pain, humiliation, sorrows, and heartaches of hundreds of children. But, for a long time I was mostly an observer, a consoler, and a sympathizer. I was good at giving advice in response journals, especially on all the boy-girl stuff I received and still receive. But looking back, I know I missed many opportunities to validate their feelings, to share a bit of my own pain with them, or to pick up on clues of abuse and hardship hidden in their anger.

Then, the pain in my own life forced me to come to grips with deep personal distress, and my appreciation for the distress of others grew. In the hope that I might help others through their pain, I set out to learn all I could about how people — children and adults — come to deal with loss and hurt. I listened to the stories of other teachers as well and learned from their experiences. I know a lot more than I used to, but I am still just a parent and a regular classroom teacher. My credentials are simply that I am learning how to recognize and cope with the effects of serious social problems on the lives of people in schools. I hope this book will help other classroom teachers do the same.

It is not a collection of learned essays, nor does it pretend to touch all the problems any teacher or parent might face. It arises out of a specific school, in a specific area. However, my reading and the knowledge I have about other places have convinced me that most North American schools experience similar problems. Circumstances, school cultures, and the ways specific problems show themselves will surely be different in different areas. But the human suffering and the human needs will be the same.

No matter where they live — Canada/United States, east/west, city/country — many children are lost, lonely, scared, and full of hurt. Some consider suicide. Some cry in washrooms. They live in a plastic, junk-food society with easy access to violence and pornography, surrounded by stressed-out adults. Not nice, but real. Most teachers do not live in that world but they recognize the new reality and they have warm hearts. When I offered to help implement a coping program in a small school, I asked for six volunteers to work with the children and got ten. After these teachers were trained, they gave daily after school time for twelve weeks. They cared that much.

The seriousness and pervasiveness of the problems this book deals with are demonstrated by the statistics. Statistical information I had used for my workshops proved outdated when I began work on the articles and again when I wrote the book. As an example, between 1988 and 1991 teenage suicide jumped fourfold in Ontario, and I am sure it is still on the increase. In the end, I did not bother trying to make sure the statistics I used were the latest available or that they covered the whole of North America — in any case, they would have been wrong within months. The most important statistics for teachers and parents are those that record the situation in and around their own community. Many will do their own research as they need it.

The same is true for the topic bibliographies. The books and articles I list have served me well, but I recognize that a lot more information on these topics has appeared recently and will continue to appear until the problems they deal with go away.

The sequence of the chapters is somewhat arbitrary, since the problems they describe are dealt with as separate issues — although I realize, of course, how often they are related. Nevertheless, the organization of the book has a logic that emerged in the writing and editing of the chapters. As I struggled with the topics, it became clear to me that, no matter what the specific situation, certain behavior (or changes in behavior) are common to most children who are hurting.

- Their schoolwork suffers.
- They show a lot of anxiety.
- They daydream or cry frequently for no apparent reason.
- They become withdrawn or abusive.
- They do not eat or sleep properly.

It also dawned on me that these cues, and the hurting they indicate, often stem from the same emotion: anger. So it made sense that a chapter on anger should come first, to give an overview of the societal pressures that affect so many of today's families, and to help parents and teachers recognize the serious or potentially serious problems their children may be facing. Listening is the other side of that coin. When people notice behaviors that suggest a child might be hurting, the first thing they have to do is *listen*, to discover if there really is a problem and, if so, what it might be. Listening is the foundation from which teachers and parents can build whatever support the child needs.

Part I, therefore, lays the basis for the rest of the book by discussing anger and listening.

Part II describes problems arising from a personal loss of some kind due to physical or sexual abuse, serious illness, death, suicide, or separation and divorce.

Part III describes the possible impact on schools of some serious social problems: alcoholism, poverty, racism, sexism, and sexuality. All of these regularly appear in our schools in some form.

Part IV, for me, is the heart of the book. Self-esteem is the keystone for every child. It is the basis of all the good feelings and good relationships that healthy, stable children enjoy. It is essential, if hurting children are to become strong, emotionally secure adults.

For many people, this book will provide an immediate resource for those days when they find themselves suddenly faced with a severely hurt child. Others may read it right through. Some may find it a depressing book, but it was not written by a depressed person. I am far from depressed. I love to quote from Erma Bombeck's book on children with cancer. "Hope has offspring, like any other animal. They are called hopelets. You don't keep them, you share them with other people who need them."

This book is a kind of hopelet. It is informational; you will learn what the children are experiencing and feeling. It is practical; you will find a number of coping strategies. And it is curricular; your students will benefit from your raised awareness and your desire to make a positive difference.

From me to you, then, comes this hopelet. Together, we *can* make a difference.

Rustico, PEI
July, 1992

PART I

Anger

The evidence of anger has been around for as long as I have been teaching, but I am noticing it more. For some time, I have been noticing anger expressed in the playground and in the office discipline binder that contains reports of children who have been sent in for fighting. I also hear it in teachers' voices as I walk by some classrooms.

We do not seem to understand or accept anger — either our own or that of our students. We punish children for showing their anger, but I see little positive effort being made to change anger-based behavior. Lectures, detentions, and suspensions are ineffective and may produce even greater anger. I think I understand why former students sometimes return to their school to vandalize it.

A counselor friend told me that we do not understand or deal well with anger anywhere in our culture, not just in schools. Newspapers and news magazines are filled with reports of violence. The next time you have occasion to watch a crowd, look at the faces. Anger is often written in frowns, tightness, and the bitter look of unhappiness. It is a known fact that anger is at the root of many societal problems like physical, sexual, and psychological abuse.

What I'm most concerned about is the anger I find in our schools. One year one of my grade eight students wrote in her journal that she had become really angry because no one at home appreciated how much effort she had given to writing her novel — she had ripped the ten typewritten pages into bits! This same student was being treated for ulcers; her rage had turned inward.

Why did this girl tear up her own painstakingly typed pages? What causes a parent or teacher to "lose it" with a child? What life situations trigger our own anger? We need to recognize the roots of anger and learn to deal with them.

The roots of anger

There are some physiological reasons for anger — for instance, it is part of our "alert" mechanism for recognizing and dealing with danger. But most of the annoyances that produce anger are linked to the behavior of other human beings. As social activist and author June Callwood puts it: "Adults lose their tempers for the same reasons babies do, for matters of domination, interference, a blow to the sense of self or not getting enough approval, support or affection."

Abandonment

Newborns show their discomfort by crying and,

if their crying does not result in attention, it intensifies into rage. Children soon realize that their comfort, even their very existence, is in the hands of others. When they imagine what might happen to them if their parents or caregivers stop looking after their needs, they begin to fear separation and abandonment. This fear is proof of our human need to belong, our dependence on others. And because we need others as we do, any perceived or feared separation becomes a blow to our emotional selves, a blow capable of triggering anger.

Disapproval

Most of us remember being disciplined as children and the feeling that we were totally rejected. Discipline often feels like disapproval of the *child* rather than of the *behavior*. Instead of "I'm angry because you broke the window," we communicate "You were stupid and careless to break the window!" So, the child internalizes "I'm stupid and careless, so I'm no good."

Our fear of disapproval may socialize us to conform, but the danger is that suppressed anger may lurk just below that conformity. As two-year-olds begin to develop a sense of self, they begin to say "no" — a natural and desirable development. But if we react to each "no" with anger and with disciplinary measures that are meant to defeat the child, we may be producing anger and insecurity. And the greater the insecurity, the greater the need for retaliation. Adults and children who believe themselves unworthy and unloved are likely to strike back.

Deprivation

Human beings need proof of their value to others. For babies, that proof takes the form of being touched and experiencing affection and positive attention. The absence of these may produce a range of feelings from mild irritation to out-and-out rage. For older children, it often takes the form of "fair" treatment. How often do we hear "No fair!" from our children? It is the battle cry of adolescents. Sibling rivalry is built on it.

Children who come to us from backgrounds that have deprived them of love, support, and nurturing can carry a smoldering fury around with them all their lives. Prejudice flourishes when people feel deprived. Many fascists have used this sense of deprivation to their advantage.

Manipulation

People have been exploited, manipulated, lied to, put down, conned, and controlled. Most of us have felt our bodies react with hostility when we were put down. Think of the hundreds of small things that drain away our sense of power, of value, of wholeness, the things that lead us to feel disrespected and unsupported, that get to us as teachers, as single people, as parents, as sons, as daughters, as sisters, as brothers. We feel inept and inadequate. We are frustrated and humiliated — and angry. Add to that, children's daily exposure to the anger and violence of others. For instance, recent reports on the media link the violence observed in videos and movies and on TV to the violent behavior of many people in our society, especially young people.

15

Basic human needs

Callwood and many others have said that basic human needs must be met if our society is to reduce the anger that pervades it. Here are the needs that are generally recognized as basic beyond food and shelter.

- We all need to *have a sense of power*. If we are not given power as a matter of course, we will rebel in anger.
- We all need to *feel close to other human beings*. If this closeness is not provided naturally, we will use angry methods to achieve it. Being ignored is infuriating. Children who act out have learned that negative strokes are better than no strokes at all.
- We all need to *feel safe, cared for*, nurtured by our world and the people in it, or anger may develop.
- We all need to *have time to be individuals*, to enjoy privacy, to center on ourselves. Without time for our selves, we can lapse into apathy, which is anger turned inward.

Parents and teachers have a special need for all these things if they are to understand and support their children's needs. Parenting and teaching demand a high energy level, and we all have differing amounts of energy available. Some parents and teachers have full buckets most of the time, topped up by people who love and support them and provide enough positive strokes in their lives. Others are not so lucky. If you are the adult child of an alcoholic, for instance, or if you live in a house where there has been a loss, or even if you are unwell, then the level in your bucket may be low, with little coming in to fill it up again. Empty buckets also tend to produce anger.

Coping with anger

Children become angry when their sense of self and their belief in their own power and safety are shaken. They become angry when they are let down by the people they trust. But the anger itself is not usually the problem for the adults around them. It is the behaviors that result from the anger that make our lives difficult.

In the following chapters I will discuss some of the behaviors you might find and some of the coping strategies you might use when anger is a component of a known or suspected problem. For now, I want to suggest some general coping strategies you can use even if you do not know the basis of the anger.

Expressed anger

When we encounter children in the classroom or on the playground who are verbally frothing at us in anger, we know that something in their environment has triggered this reaction. Perhaps they are projecting the hurts of home onto us. Perhaps we have ridiculed or embarrassed them. Perhaps friends have baited them or the work has frustrated them. Whatever the cause, they have blown up. What can we do?

First and foremost, we must not let their anger trigger our own. Barbara Coloroso, noted lecturer and writer, warns us not to get pulled into becoming that angry six-year-old we all feel like at times. Here are some of her coping suggestions.

- Center your own energy.
- Dissipate aggressiveness by lowering your voice.
- Work for a win-win situation. Say: "Wow, you're

really angry. You are welcome to . . . until you cool off." Options could include stepping outside, walking to the end of the hall and back, staying but fuming quietly.

- Believe in yourself and maintain your personal dignity. Believe in the children and their sense of personal dignity.
- Find something positive to say when the children have calmed down. For example, "I like the way you . . ."

Here are more ideas from Violet Oaklander, former teacher and child therapist.

- Acknowledge that the anger is okay but the behavior is not.
- Acquaint the children with alternative ways of dealing with anger: tearing newspaper, wadding paper, kicking a pillow, kicking a can, running around the block, hitting a bed with a tennis racket, yelling in the shower, writing, drawing, pounding clay, etc.
- Discuss anger openly, both individually and in class sessions. What is it? What makes us angry? How do we deal with it? How do people know we're angry?
- Role-play expressing anger.

From my own experience I would add that it is important to seek privacy with the child as quickly as possible. Children are likely to calm down a lot better when they are not confronted by the stares and comments of their peers.

Unexpressed anger

What about children who hold their anger in? What about all the girls and women, especially, who have been socialized into believing that nice girls do not slam, bang, or shout? I was brought up with: "Take that look off your face" and "Don't you dare talk back to me."

Females tend to hide their anger by turning it inward. They become depressed or the energy of their anger goes underground, surfacing in criticism, sarcasm, or general dissatisfaction with life. A lot of hostility can be disguised as barbed teasing as well, and sometimes it's difficult to be aware of it and stop it.

In our school, the girls often just stand around at recess in all-girl groups, except for a few who play a bit of tag with the boys or engage in attempts at girl-boy contact. The boys, on the other hand, participate in active, aggressive games that help them to release their hostility and anger.

Helping children express their anger

I wish people could learn to express their anger in good and meaningful ways. I believe that every school should have a rage room, for instance, where angry children can batter plastic punching bags and stuffed toys and not each other. One day I saw a grade eight girl stomping down the hall toward the library. When I caught up with her she looked at me and snarled, "I've got to go and pound Papa Smurf or I'll pound Julie instead." I told her to go ahead. Papa Smurf can take it.

I believe that angry students should not be sent to the office, but to someone in the building who will listen, validate their anger, and help them come up with strategies to cope with it. I believe that everyone who works with children should take stock of their own biases, prejudices, trigger points, and ways of dealing with anger. I believe that we should take our emotional temperature each morning and periodically throughout the day. There's nothing wrong with saying to kids, "I'm in a pretty bad mood today, so walk softly." There's everything right about apologizing to a student on whom we have vented hostility brought in from another life situation.

I wish all teachers and parents could look behind the symptoms of anger, aggression, and rebellion and try to ascertain the underlying cause. We cannot change children's lives, but we can help them to understand their own anger and develop their own ways of improving their outlook on life.

I do not want to live in a world where more societal stresses lead to more unresolved anger. We have a role to play. We need to accept an individual sense of responsibility for seeking to understand and accept others. We need to commit ourselves to helping create a better life in our own homes and schools, for the sake of our students. As Barbara Coloroso says: "Kids are worth it."

Anger

CHILDREN: THE CHALLENGE, Rudolf Dreikurs and Vicki Soltz, Dutton, 1991.

EMOTIONS: WHAT THEY ARE AND HOW THEY AFFECT US, June Callwood, Doubleday, 1986.

DISCIPLINE: CREATING A POSITIVE SCHOOL CLIMATE, Barbara Coloroso, Video and audio cassettes, Kids Are Worth It!, 1990. (Other Kids Are Worth It! materials listed in Appendix).

THE HURRIED CHILD, David Elkind, Addison Wesley, 1988.

WINDOWS TO OUR CHILDREN: A GESTALT THERAPY APPROACH TO CHILDREN AND ADOLESCENTS, Violet Oaklander, Gestalt Journal, 1989.

LISTENING

Listen

When I ask you to listen to me and
you start giving me advice . . .
you have not done what I asked.
When I ask you to listen to me and
you begin to tell me why I shouldn't
feel that way . . .
you are trampling on my feelings.
When I ask you to listen to me and
you feel you have to do something
to solve my problems . . .
you have failed me, strange as that may be.
Perhaps that's why prayer works for some people
Because
God is silent . . .
He doesn't offer advice
or try to fix things.
He just listens and trusts you to work it
out for yourself.
So please, just listen and hear me.
And, if you want to talk, wait a few minutes
for your turn and
I promise
I will listen to you.
   Anonymous

Most of us have done the things this poem mentions: we give advice, "own" other people's problems, or tell them that their feelings are wrong, confused or illogical. How often do we really *hear* what others are saying?

Most people listen carefully, really listen, only a small percentage of the time. In fact, it would be impossible to attend to all the talk that surrounds us. It has been estimated that we spend one-third of our waking hours listening to verbal messages from people around us and from radio and television. That's more than five hours of talk each day. And don't overlook the chatterbox in our own heads that keeps us posted about our personal concerns. Undeniably, we live in a world of aural distractions.

For our own sanity, we have to let our attention wander occasionally. Wanting to be polite to the person speaking to us, we nod from time to time, utter an occasional "Oh?" or "Um-hmmm," and pick up on the last three words for a comment. Sometimes the talk we hear threatens or frightens us, and then we block it out completely or change the topic, because we simply cannot cope. On the other hand, lovers hang on each other's every word. When job, health, well-being, and loved ones are the topic, words become crucial. We listen intensely and afterward often find ourselves emotionally and physically drained.

The need for good listening

Often, the first crucial step in helping hurting children is simply listening to them — really listening. And we listen best when we offer empathy, recognize the problems or concerns, sense the deep feelings and try to learn what the children need, both immediately and in the future. What they say may make you want to run right out and "fix" their world, but that is something you can seldom do. Be prepared, initially, to use your listening skills simply to say, in effect: "Help me to understand what it is to be you right now."

Sometimes you might share a bit of yourself as well. If the children know about some of your pain and disappointment, they may feel freer to share their own. Sharing yourself is not easy, however. It takes being secure in your own skin and knowing who you are and what you value and believe. It also takes being aware of the power that comes with your role as teacher or parent as well as confidant.

Whether you share your own feelings or not, good listening can and should accept and validate the children's: "It's okay to feel that way." Good listening is the foundation of good counseling, and good counseling will help children see their own strengths. It will provide information that will help them make good choices. It may provide an outside view of themselves in their difficult situation and perhaps help them change their perception of things. For the moment, you may be the only person who can do these things for them . . . if you listen carefully. Committed, skilled, empathetic, and kind listening builds trust — the keystone of any effective helping relationship.

Psychologists who have researched how children from dysfunctional families became fully functioning citizens have discovered that those children have usually met someone who believed in them, one person who said something similar to what I once said to one of my delinquent and disorderly female students: "You of my delinquent and disorderly female students: "You want to be a truckdriver like your dad? If you drop out, can you do it? I'm counting on you to walk into my school in a few years and say, 'Hey, Mrs. Newman, I made it.' "

We all want our students to live productive and worthwhile lives, even — perhaps especially — the obnoxious ones, the hurting ones, the twisted ones. "But they won't talk to me!" you say. "They just sit there and glare defiantly at me!" They *will* come to talk if they know you will listen. So will the lost, lonely, withdrawn ones; the proud, snotty ones; the leave-me-alone ones. If you show sincere care by really listening, you will reach the core way-down-deep inside them. Once trust is there, so will be the relief of having someone to understand them and be on their side.

Poor listeners

Adler and Town have suggested ways to recognize poor listening. There are various types.

Pseudo-listeners

These counterfeit listeners erect a facade of politeness to mask their own thoughts.

Stage-hoggers

Me-too listeners keep jumping into our talk with their own stories, interpretations, and reactions.

Selective listeners

They respond only to those parts of our talk that interest them and tune out the rest. We are all selective listeners in some situations. We listen selectively when small children chatter on and on; it would be too impractical to do anything else. Some adults prefer response — it is their own telling they enjoy. But selective listening in the situations this book describes will usually be poor listening.

Insulated listeners

They use repression and denial mechanisms to filter out the speech they do not want to hear. Children are masters at it: "In one ear and out the other."

Defensive listeners

They take most of what is said as a personal attack. Parents and teachers of teenagers have lots of experience with them.

Ambushers

Some people wait to pounce on you to turn your words against you. Trial lawyers make their living this way. Teenagers, who consider their parents pretty stupid, are good at it, too. Siblings love it.

Insensitive listeners

They make no attempt to look beyond the words for feelings or hidden meanings.

Spotting poor listening is not always easy, especially if you do not know the person well. In our multicultural society, even lack of eye contact may not tell you, since eye contact is an insult in some cultures. The more you know a person, of course, the more you will be able to tell the quality of his or her listening.

How to become an effective listener

First, try to understand and recognize poor listening, perhaps using Adler and Town's list. Above all, learn to assess your own listening. Teachers and parents are especially prone to jump in with advice when dealing with children. I remember saying too often to my own children, "When I was your age . . . ," when what they needed was for me to hear — really hear — *their* concerns. By jumping in I told them, "I'm not really interested."

Next, learn to become an active listener. Active listening says: "I'd like to solve your problem for you, but I can't. What I can do is help you try to find a solution for yourself." Active listening removes the burden of having to be all-knowing; instead, the listener helps the speaker clarify his or her own mind and encourages deeper levels of understanding. Successful active listening requires a sincere desire to help and a willingness to trust. It takes time. It takes acceptance that the child's thoughts, words, and feelings are right for him or her at the moment.

The mechanics of active listening

- Try to make the setting right — same eye level, a private place.
- Keep your own talk to a minimum.
- Show your attention through your body. Turn toward the child and do nothing else at the same time. Encourage with nods, murmurs, and the odd word of understanding.
- Have tissues handy.
- Every so often, check back to be sure you understand what is being said. Do not parrot the child's words but rephrase them. For instance, "It sounds as though . . ." "You're telling me that . . ." "I get the feeling that you . . ." "I hear you saying that . . ."
- If the child wanders away from the issue, keep com-

ing back to the main concern: "You were telling me
about . . ."

- Listen for feelings behind the words: "You seem to
be pretty angry/sad/confused . . ." The child will
either nod: "She understands me!" or correct you:
"No, I'm not mad. I want to cry."

Listening questions

Alfred Benjamin, a leading authority on listening
skills, suggests that listeners often ask too many questions or questions that confuse and interrupt the talker.
If our questions take control of the child's train of
thought, then we become the big authority figure, the
expert. Our goal must be for the child to share what is
inside. A warm, positive relationship cannot develop if
the child feels challenged and hemmed in by questions.

Benjamin describes both some discouraging and
some encouraging questions.

Closed questions

"You're tired, aren't you?" "Don't you want to
learn this?" "Do you like school?" Closed questions *dis-
courage* by inviting a specific, often one-word answer.
They keep the communication door firmly shut.

Open questions

"How are you feeling after so much exercise?"
"You don't seem yourself. Did something happen?"
"This subject can be difficult. What is the hardest part
for you?" "Some people like school and others aren't so
keen. How about you?" Questions like these *encourage*
by soliciting views, opinions, thoughts, and feelings.
They invite wider and deeper contact.

Mixed-message questions

"You don't want that cookie, do you?" "She shouldn't run so fast, should she?" "You didn't mean to hit him. You were tired, right?" These *discouraging* questions imply agreement and require no answer.

Double questions

"Do you want to do it now or later?" "Do you want to sit with John or Judy?" Preschoolers respond well to double questions, and they can help children become better decision-makers. But in counseling conversations they are discouraging because they limit choices.

Bombarding (hailstone) questions

"Why don't you speak up? Did you hear me? Wasn't I clear enough?" "Who hit you? When? Where?" Certainly I don't like questions like these coming at me. Give me a chance to catch my breath! Give *me* some control! Very *discouraging*.

Direct questions

"Why didn't you do this?" "How is life at home?" These can be *discouraging*, since they put children under pressure to respond.

Indirect questions

These are more gentle: "It must be tough doing all those decimal questions." "I'm wondering how things are for you just now." "You must have some thoughts on . . ." "I'd like to hear about . . ." Indirect questions are an encouraging way of showing interest without pressure.

Children, especially teenagers, hate snooping, nosy adults, which we become when we keep butting in to their private business to "have a talk" with them, or when a topic they initiate leads into personal things they are not willing to share. Yet you often need to understand what is going on. You need to ask questions when you have not heard right or understood, for whatever reason. You need to ask children to repeat things so you know that they understand what you have said. You may need to help them clarify or explore a thought or feeling: "What did you mean by . . .?" You also need questions, sometimes, to bridge an awkward gap or fill a silence.

Naturally, I am delighted to encounter children who open up without a lot of effort on my part. More often, though, I have to probe gently. I might ask: "If you had three wishes about your class/your friends/your family, what would they be?" "What's one thing you would change about . . . if you had a magic wand?" "Tell me three good things and three not-so-good things about your life right now." "Sometimes kids who have gone through what you are going through right now feel . . . . How about you?" I'm really saying: "I want to understand. Tell me about . . ."

I have also learned to limit my whys. "Why" often implies disapproval and invites defensiveness, withdrawal, or attack: "Why did you do that?" "Because . . ." There is no meaningful reply since the question points to a hidden criticism: "Shape up!" Children know from experience that if the reply is not carefully considered, punishment may be imminent.

Ironically, most of us do not really know why we do things most of the time. Nor will some children be willing to share the real reason with us, the authority figures, even if they do know. Often they don't know why, are trying to figure out why, or don't wish to tell why. "Why did you hit her?" "Because she's taken my place as an only child and I'm jealous." They say nothing, or "Because," or what they think you want them to say. Listen to them in class, in the principal's office, or on the playground. "He hit me first." "She made me." "He started it." Instead of asking why, we might do better to invite the children to tell us their version of what happened, "the facts" as they see them.

There is a place for advice if the child asks you for it. We all sometimes want to sink into the comfort of allowing someone to "do it" for us, of having someone tell us that this crisis, too, will pass. But too often children expect us to fix their problems. They want solutions, especially when the situations they face seem overwhelming: "Who will I live with, Mom or Dad?" They expect us to relieve their anxiety and make intensely personal decisions for them. They expect us to tell them how to be popular, how to end loneliness. They may count on a wave of our counseling wand to make all the bad stuff go away.

Unfortunately, we cannot fix their lives. All we can say is, "What are your choices?" Often I get a blank stare when I ask that question. So I continue: "Well, one choice is to hit back. Or you could . . .?" I encourage further thinking until, together, we have come up with five choices, one for each finger on one hand. Then the child decides which one to try, knowing that if it does not work, there are four more. We need to show children problem-solving in action, but in the end they must take ownership of the behavior.

Try to suggest strategies that are appropriate for the child and the situation. For instance:

- Encourage a child who has a big decision to make to write two lists detailing the good things and bad things about each choice. Lists like this have helped teenagers decide which parent to live with.
- Suggest: "If you can't say what you want to say to your father (or mother or both), could you write a letter and leave it on the table in the morning?" Several students have had success with this strategy.
- Suggest a totally personal journal, one that no one else will ever see. I have had children leave their personal notebooks with me for safekeeping during the summer months.
- There is even a place for, "I can't know exactly how you feel, but once when I had something similar happen, what worked for me was . . ."

Give children who need help the gift of your time, attention, and knowledge. If a child arrives at your door frantic to share when you have other pressing matters, there is nothing wrong with saying, "I have to be somewhere in ten minutes, but if you talk while I clean up these papers, I'll listen as best I can." However, in normal circumstances, try to give them what you would want a counselor or friend to give *you* if you needed help sorting out your own tough circumstances. Let me share my own list.

- I would want someone to listen with understanding, not only to my words, but also to my body language and to the feelings behind the words. The mere telling of my tale would already be therapeutic.
- I would not want the "Um-hmm"s and the "So I

hear you saying . . ." statements to be mere techniques. I don't think a person who is unwilling to share some of his or her own pain and confusion could help me much.

• On the other hand, if my listener and I simply swapped pain stories would I end up being helped enough? I need more than a fellow traveler along troubled roads.

• I would want my listener to be wise and skillful in interpreting what I say. I need someone who can bring all the bits and pieces of my conversation together and unveil for me the things I haven't been able to see or understand about myself and my situation.

• I wouldn't necessarily want precise advice but I would welcome hearing about options that might work. Perhaps it's options that I most need.

Helping children depends on using your active listening skills so your expertise and knowledge can be brought to bear. You may not think you have that expertise, but when you are faced with a needy child who looks to you for help, when you want to help that child with all your heart, rest assured that you have more skills than you think you have and an inner wisdom to rely on. Trust that wisdom to assist children in coping with difficult circumstances. They will learn a lot of valuable life skills in the process. And remember, your essential contribution does not lie in the choice of precise technique, but in your caring and commitment. Children sense the presence of caring. Parents sense it too.

There are limits

Unfortunately, concern and commitment aren't always enough. Sometimes, no matter how much you care and try, no matter how effective your active listening skills may be, you will fail.

Today's world is filled with anger, and too many of our students are caught in the effects of it — not only in their own anger, not only in the anger of those close to them who may have power over them, but also in the anger of social prejudice and fear. Unfortunately, we do not handle anger well in our homes, in our schools, or in our culture as a whole. In fact, anger is the basis of most of the problems this book describes, and you will find the word used frequently.

As a result, children sometimes get caught in problems that require better solutions than they can muster alone or with your help. The following chapters describe some painful personal and social problems our students bring to or meet in school. To help these children, you may have to draw on all the behavior management and conflict resolution courses you've taken, on all the articles and books you've read, on the resurces listed in this book, and perhaps on expert help from the school or community. And all you may have in the end is your faith in human resilience in the face of overwhelming odds.

Listening

Resources for Adults

CREATIVE CONFLICT RESOLUTION: MORE THAN 200 ACTIVITIES FOR KEEPING PEACE IN THE CLASSROOM, William J. Kreidler, Scott Foresman, 1984.

THE HELPING INTERVIEW, Alfred Benjamin, Houghton Mifflin, 1981.

HOW TO TALK SO KIDS WILL LISTEN, AND LISTEN SO KIDS WILL TALK, Adele Faber and Elaine Maslish, Avon, 1982.

KIDS CAN COOPERATE: A PRACTICAL GUIDE TO TEACHING PROBLEM SOLVING, Elizabeth Crary, Parenting Press, 1984.

LETTERS TO JUDY: WHAT YOUR KIDS WISH THEY COULD TELL YOU, Judy Blume, Putnam, 1986.

LOOKING OUT, LOOKING IN: INTERPERSONAL COMMUNICATION, Ron Adler and Neil Towne, Holt, Rinehart & Winston, 1990.

Resources for Children

DEAR DOCTOR ... TEENAGERS ASK ABOUT, Dr. Saul Levine and Dr. Kathleen Wilcox, Lothrop, Kids Can Press, 1987. (grade 7 and up)

DOUBLE-DIP FEELINGS: A BOOK TO HELP CHILDREN UNDERSTAND EMOTIONS, Barbara S. Cain, Magination Press, 1991. (ages 4-8)

PART II

PHYSICAL ABUSE

*She's a friend, a small, lovely, deeply spiritual woman.
"When he threw me against the bedroom wall and I began
sliding down," she said, "something in me said that this was
the moment for me to go." She went out into the night, called
her babysitting daughter from a pay phone and told her
where she was. When the daughter joined her on the street
corner, they called a friend who took them in. She has never
gone back.*

●●●●●

*"It was one thing when he beat me," another friend said, "but
when he started choking my son, I couldn't stay any longer."
Ten years after her divorce, she still has nightmares about the
beatings.*

●●●●●

*Two children came off the bus weeping in terror. The father
had been so abusive that they were afraid to go home that
night. The school called the social service agency and a social
worker accompanied them home.*

●●●●●

A teacher sent a little primary boy to see me in my role as school counselor. Bright and articulate, he openly described a father who kicked his mom, who threw heavy objects and yelled obscenities, who punched and slapped. He told me of going with his mother to the shelter for battered wives, how there were not many toys there, how his daddy was sorry and took them home. But nothing had changed and now his mother said she was leaving, getting an apartment. After he left, I sat still for a long time.

During a second meeting, I asked him if home things ever bothered him at school. He replied that sometimes he thought about home and felt like throwing up. During the violence, he and his smaller sister would hide under the bed, or make themselves very small on the living room couch underneath a blanket. Once his mother sent him out of the house for help. A nearby store owner said he could not leave his store because a customer might come in. So the boy stood out on the street and screamed. As we talked, his fingers kept twisting, twisting. Soon he left the school, and the local paper reported that his father had been jailed.

Many children in our schools are physically abused — punched, hit on the head, kicked, shoved, jabbed. Others have to watch their mothers or siblings being beaten.

More and more is being done to help people recognize the reality of physical abuse, stop it, and cope with its effects. Provincial or state and local school jurisdictions are disseminating information about the topic to teachers.

A family violence prevention brochure counsels: "Children from violent families are in our schools. As educators, we have a responsibility to these children. Children exposed to family violence often face major adjustment problems during childhood and adolescence — and are themselves more prone to become batterers or victims. We do not want that cycle to continue."

Abused women

Here are some recent findings.

- One in ten women is abused by her partner.
- Fifteen percent of all homicide victims are women murdered by their partners.
- An alarming percentage of pregnant women are attacked.
- One in three fathers who batter their wives also hit their children.
- Mothers who are battered hit their children in turn.
- Boys who come from a home where a mother was beaten are likely to become batterers themselves.
- Children who witness violence can be as profoundly affected as those who are themselves beaten.

What kind of men abuse women? (Very few women abuse men.) They come from all professions and seem like normal men in every other respect. They are not mentally ill. Doctors, bricklayers, lawyers, fishermen, teachers. . . any man could be on the list. What they have in common is some combination of the following attitudes and actions.

- Their behavior is learned.

- They control by fear and threats, and assault verbally as well as physically.
- They are intensely jealous.
- They accuse their victims of provoking them.
- They often experience personality shifts, to the point of denying and forgetting beatings.
- They become enraged without provocation or at the slightest "misbehavior" of those they batter.
- They may become more violent when the woman is pregnant or just after she gives birth. Babies have been born bruised.
- They are very remorseful after the violence, promising their victims the moon if they will forgive them.
- They have a strong belief in male superiority, yet personally have low self-esteem.
- They express most emotion as anger and feel a great sense of isolation.
- They usually are not violent outside the family.

Why do women stay with such men? Remember the old saying: "Do it to me once and it's your fault. Do it twice and it's my fault." Why do women not take their children and leave these men after the first assault? The question seems simple, but the answer is not. Here are a few of the complexities:

- Many women do not have the financial resources to leave.
- They do not know where to go; there are never enough shelters to provide a safe place for battered women and their children.
- The violence builds bit by bit.
- The women feel ashamed to show their bruises and cuts.

- Once they have vented their rage, the men are apologetic and promise never to do it again, and the women believe them, perhaps because they continue to love their partner's better side.
- Some women stay because in their culture it is "normal" to experience battering.
- Some women have even said that the wonderful loving and caring afterward makes the assault worth it.
- Some violent men are good fathers, and the family unit means a lot to them, as well as to the mothers.

What makes me saddest of all is meeting women who, after a lot of abusive treatment, have become emotionally dependent on their abusers. They suffer personality changes, exhibit erratic behavior, become depressed, and require sedatives. They lose the ability to make simple decisions, and to love, nurture, and protect their children. They become women without hope, with abysmally low self-esteem, and women who are socialized into believing they are nothing without a man.

Abused children

Spanking

Faith in spanking is widespread. In vain, I once tried to convince a grade seven class that there are better ways to bring up children than by spanking them into "better persons." I even called on my principal to support my arguments. He explained why the strap has been banned in schools, and described our school's problem-solving techniques to deal with misdemeanors. But neither of us made much of an impact on that class.

The incident reminded me that my own beliefs used to be very different. My father, a gentle man, never once raised his hand to my sister and me. However, my mother disciplined enough for two parents, using her slipper as a spanking tool. In turn, I used to spank my own five children. (Parents tend to raise their children the way they were raised, unless taught otherwise.) But several years ago I put two questions to myself and decided I would never spank another child. Those questions were:

- What is the line between spanking and beating, between fair and judicial physical discipline and physical assault?
- Does spanking do any good? Does pain really stop any unwelcome behavior or train a child in anything but fear?

Beyond spanking

Still, some parents believe that sparing the rod will spoil the child. I meet many children who tell me about the war zone they call home — the yelling, the sibling fights, the parental arguments. Clearly, some parents physically lash out at any misbehavior, at any sign of disobedience, or at any inability of the child to understand. Clearly, too, their children suffer more than spanking.

Abusive homes are anything but easy to understand, as author Shea J. Gold makes clear. She mentions the existence of a parent/infant "toxicity syndrome": deficiencies of nutrients in parents and/or children that may cause nervousness, irritability, extreme fatigue, and a tendency toward hyperaggressive, short-fuse behavior. She presents profiles of low-risk and high-risk mothers (potential batterers), as well as low- and high-risk children. High-risk children might include those who have been exposed to lead poisoning, who have minor undetected infections, or who experienced some sort of brain damage at birth.

The number of infant deaths from abuse in the first few months of life is high. This is especially the case for babies who are cranky or who won't go to sleep. Here is a common pattern for an abused baby: premature or underweight and born to a young mother who had a stressful pregnancy but who wants to keep this little doll who is so loving and so much hers. Already the stresses have begun. Another peak occurs during the two-year-old period when children are trying to assert themselves.

Gold reveals a number of other patterns, often linked to nutrition and health. She also describes the psychologies of abused children. An overwhelming percentage of prison inmates, for example, were abused children. As many as 70 percent of children who survive abuse will show marked physical or developmental deviations.

She believes that battered children develop a need to provoke punishment wherever they go. Some children will seek to substitute a tolerable physical pain for unbearable emotional pain. Ironically, abused children often become bullies in the schoolyard. Most children from violent homes end up believing that it is okay to hit women, that violence is a way to win arguments, that adults have power they often misuse, that men are bullies who push women and other men around, and that women are victims who cannot take care of themselves and their children.

Abused children in school

Let us look in detail at some of the children we teach who see violence at home and experience it on their own bodies.

In general, they all experience great anxiety, confusion, and terror of being abandoned. I see disturbing patterns being lived out in pre-adolescent and adolescent girls who hand in journals with pages full of longing for this or that boy. They become stricken with grief and panic when a boy breaks off their relationship; many have their second and third choices already in mind, anxious to fill any void.

When I talk about family violence, some girls get very indignant, stating categorically that no guy will ever lay a hand on them. But when I observe the value they set on "going with" a boy, I fear that they will come to use the same rationalizations older women do: "He didn't really mean it." "I shouldn't have done what I did." "I made him mad." "It was my fault." Girls already in this pattern who also see their fathers hit their mothers, or who are being hit themselves, will internalize a victim role. In some families, children blame the mother for her weakness. Young sons soon verbally and then physically abuse her also. The whole family gets caught up in a web of anger, remorse, and guilt.

We are teaching these children. We are teaching youngsters who already use physical means to solve problems, aggressive students who do not deal with stress in a reasonable manner and who do not show empathy with or sympathy for their peers. It is easy to spot students who see aggression as a way of life, who idealize violence in their art and writing, and who cheer on playground fighters. We also need to spot the ones who try to hide or who flinch away from our touch. Sometimes we can encourage these children to tell us about their fear. More often, we have to find the clues in their behaviors and attitudes.

Preschoolers up to age five
   These children may experience:

- physical complaints such as stomach aches, headaches, sleep disturbances, heightened fear of the dark, resistance to bedtime, and, in school, excessive tiredness
- excessive separation anxieties, indicated by whining and clinging
- failure to thrive when they enter school

School-age children six to twelve
   These children may:

- become seductive or manipulative as a way of reducing tension
- hang around home a lot, believing their presence will protect the mom — or the exact opposite, stay away as much as possible
- become insecure and distrustful of their environment, especially if there are frequent unpredictable parental separations
- fear being abandoned
- fear their own anger or the anger of others
- fear being killed or killing someone else
- exhibit eating disorders such as overeating, under-eating, or hoarding food

Adolescents

Because adolescence is a stressful time for any child, the feelings are even more acute for this group. They may:

- escape into drug or alcohol abuse
- run away from home
- escape into pregnancy and early marriage
- suffer suicidal or homicidal thoughts and actions
- become involved in criminal activities such as drug dealing, theft, and assault

Watch for extremes of behavior in any age group. Some children will show impaired concentration spans, difficulty with school work, poor attendance at school, or clumsy, accident-prone behavior. Others, especially an oldest child, may show the opposite: excellent academic work, perfectionist standards (harboring a tremendous fear of failure), and a strong sense of responsibility.

I think of the children who stand stiff as a board when I try to hug them, or those who start when I pat an arm. I think of the ones who believe their family is like all others or who cover up bruises and cuts with clothing. I think of the little ones who pipe up in "show and tell" how Daddy hit Mommy last night and she cried — but who will soon learn about the code of silence. I think of the children who still have an aching love for the adult who abuses them.

Someone who has spent years working with street kids in a large city once told me that teens run *away*, not *to* — away from intolerable circumstances at home, most often physical abuse, sexual abuse, and excrutiating emotional abuse. Unfortunately, the "to" too often leads to self-destructive activities such as heavy drug use and prostitution. For most of these children, no adult — relative, neighbor, teacher, guidance counselor — was available to hear their fearful stories.

What can we do?

If you suspect or know about abuse at home, you need to call for intervention and help. But effective help is not always easy to arrange. In my area, the social service agency needs bruises or convincing evidence that the children are viewing battering before it can act on behalf of children .

The process of intervention can also be frustrating. I hear stories of the inability of agencies to act fast enough or long enough. Sometimes, when agencies are called in, families move away. Social workers are faced with large case loads. Counseling sessions are often up to six weeks apart, and the family drops out or otherwise slips through the cracks.

Yet, as I say when I give workshops, warm hearts can make a difference. A surprisingly large number of children become normal, successful adults despite stressful, disadvantaged, and even brutalized childhoods. Michael Rutter, a British psychiatrist, says that certain school conditions help foster success. He lists these important factors for resiliency.

- a positive sense of self-esteem and self-worth
- a feeling of control over at least some things
- security in one or more relationships
- adaptability to changing circumstances
- social problem-solving skills

School is not just a setting for pedagogy, Rutter believes, but also a social organization that provides an opportunity for social learning. Teachers who demonstrate successful coping with their own stress give important messages to children. Children who do not become carbon copies of the abuser or the victim generally have had good experiences at school — not necessarily on the academic side, but perhaps in other areas such as sports and music. Two factors are especially helpful: a good relationship with one or more teachers and a position of responsibility within the school.

How else can we help? We can foster trust in hurting children so they come to look on us as someone who sincerely cares. In our classrooms, playgrounds, libraries, gyms, and hallways, children must always be treated with respect and dignity, with fairness and concern. Discipline is necessary, but rigidity is not. Structure is essential, but rudeness is inexcusable.

Show you care for the hurting children caught in a web of anger and violence and fear. Learn all you can about physical abuse to expand your own awareness and knowledge, and, above all, watch and listen. Stress problem-solving strategies. Learn how to recognize anger and how to guide it into constructive paths. Help make school a safe place, a sanctuary — perhaps for some children the only caring structure they'll know. And remember, the child who is the most obnoxious may be the one who is hurting the most and who needs you the most.

Physical Abuse

Resources for Adults

"Child Abuse! The Ministry Speaks Out" in *B.C. Teacher* (Vol. 57, no. 2).

CHILDREN OF BATTERED WOMEN, Peter Jaffe, Susan Kaye Wilson and David A. Wolfe, Sage Publications, 1990.

NATIONAL CHILD ABUSE HOT-LINE 1-800-4-A-CHILD (U.S.) NATIONAL CLEARINGHOUSE ON CHILD ABUSE & NEGLECT
P.O. Box 1182
Washington, D.C. 20013
(703) 821-2086

"Resilient Children," Michael Rutter, *Psychology Today*, March, 1984.

THUMBS DOWN: A GUIDE FOR TEACHERS (A CLASSROOM APPROACH TO FAMILY VIOLENCE), 1986. Available from:
NATIONAL CLEARINGHOUSE ON FAMILY VIOLENCE
Family Violence Prevention Division
Social Services Program Branch
Health & Welfare Canada
Ottawa, Ontario
K1A 1B5
1-800-267-1291

WHEN CHILDREN INVITE CHILD ABUSE, Svea J. Gold, Fern Ridge Press, 1986.

WORKING WITH CHILDREN FROM VIOLENT HOMES: IDEAS AND TECHNIQUES, Diane Davis, Network Publishing, 1986.

Resources for Children

DEGRASSI TALKS: ABUSE, Boardwalk Books Inc., Mint Publishers and Toronto Sun, 1992. (grades 4-12)

SOMETHING IS WRONG AT MY HOUSE, Diane Davis, Parenting Press, 1985. (ages 3-12)

SEXUAL **ABUSE**

She and her sister would be called into the bedroom by their grandfather one at a time, and he would fondle them and make them touch his penis. They didn't tell for a long time, but one day the older child couldn't keep "their secret" any longer and told the mother.

● ● ● ● ●

He was a teenage babysitter who used the late hours to molest the older girl. The younger sister eventually disclosed to help her sibling. Both girls needed counseling afterward.

● ● ● ● ●

A young boy was made to watch pornographic movies from the time he was seven until he was eleven. Then the abuser, who was a family member, turned his attention to a younger nephew, who quickly told his mother. This freed the first boy to reveal his story as well.

● ● ● ● ●

A neighbor, respected by parents who let their children play in his yard, one day took several children inside his house, undressed them and fondled them in turn. One ran home in great distress and told his parents. The man was charged.

● ● ● ● ●

One of the students who was part of that last episode kept telling his story over and over in "show and tell" and to anyone on duty at recess. The social worker told the child's teacher that he was trying to make some sense of it in his mind, a vital step towards his eventual healing. The boy feared the upcoming court case, when he would have to testify.

From my own background, I can now tell what happened to me. As a young teacher at a convention in Calgary, I was waiting in a hotel lobby for friends when a man sitting directly across from me exposed himself. I gave him the response he was after. I jumped up and left in obvious distress. I never told anyone until now.

I found this chapter difficult to write. I felt a volcano of rage and a great deal of grief for the little children who are victims of twisted sexuality. So many children are victims of sexual abuse! I remember breaking down and weeping when I made a research note about potential sex abuse victims being compliant and soft little boys and girls who need a loving human touch. I want to be Joan of Arc and take on the whole society that sets out to turn children, especially girls, into polite, quiet, cooperative students who look upon adults as gods. It is a system that allows these tender ones to be psychologically tormented and physically and sexually abused. I want to roar at parents and teachers to allow and encourage little girls to express their anger and outrage and little boys their tears and hurts.

Sexually abused children are angry. All of us, teachers and parents, need to become aware of this kind of anger and set out to help these children deal with it. If we do not, if someone does not, the girls' anger may turn into deep depression and the boys' into a drive that will produce men who dominate and abuse weaker beings.

Secrets

I sometimes scan the more than 400 faces at Monday morning assembly and wonder. Recent statistics claim that one in four girls and one in ten boys are sexually abused. Among these children in front of me I know of only a handful who are abused. How many more are suffering abuse in silence? Am I also looking at the next generation of abusers? I read somewhere that out of the average six children in any classroom who have been abused, only one or two will be willing to talk about it. My own experience tells me that there are even fewer who will tell.

I surveyed two classes, making sure that the children's answers remained anonymous. I asked:

- Has anyone ever touched you in a way that was inappropriate? (We had previously discussed what is inappropriate.)
- Has anyone ever made you touch his or her body in inappropriate places or asked you to look at those places?
- Has anyone ever asked you to show your private places to him or her?

Each question yielded affirmative answers from this group. Yet, even though I stressed the importance of disclosure to an adult they could trust, no one came forward to me or to any other teacher. Why do children keep such secrets? The answer is complex.

- Well over 50 percent of cases involve family members, friends, or other trusted adults who pressure the children not to tell.
- There is usually no violence, especially in the beginning, although there may be plenty of threats of violence against both the child and the family.
- If the children's self-esteem is already low, it is easy for the abuser to take advantage of their feelings of shame and guilt.
- Many lonely children ache to be touched, to be held, and to feel loved, important, and valued.
- Some children enjoy the pleasurable feelings and sensations that may be part of the experience.
- Others believe they are holding the family together or rescuing the abuser from unhappiness. "It's our secret" becomes the weapon of silence.

We teach our children vigilance against strangers who might kidnap and/or murder them. But many of us do not warn them to be wary of trusted loved ones who might sexually abuse them. And when it happens, often they hold the secret into adulthood. In many cases, the truth is too horrible to face and amnesia becomes a protective shield.

A new teacher came to our small Alberta school when I was a student in grade nine. All the girls developed giant crushes on this tall, handsome man with his new wife and baby. Four years later, the town hotline buzzed with the news that the teacher had been arrested for getting a young babysitter pregnant. But when they heard that he had to serve a jail sentence and was barred from ever teaching again, the town's sympathy was with him. Everyone knew she was "that kind of girl." My judgment today is much harsher than the town's was then, for he had betrayed his position of trust in the community.

For this girl, pregnancy disclosed the situation, but in many cases disclosure happens only much later or never. Our culture plays right into the hands of abusers. Children are considered miniature beings we adults must mold and shape. Disciplining them often means making them do what adults, the powerful ones, say they must do. As a result, many children feel powerless in situations where a loved or respected adult says: "Don't tell or I'll be in trouble" or ". . . you'll hurt your mother's feelings" or ". . . you'll be in trouble" or ". . . I could go to jail." Feelings of guilt overwhelm the child and the abuser hooks right into them.

Our culture openly promotes sexuality in magazines, in ads, on TV, and in movies and videos. Yet many parents do not discuss sexuality with little children — no wonder some youngsters do not know that abusing physical contact is wrong. Younger children developmentally cannot understand sex in a conscious way. When they are told later they should have asked for help at the time, they suffer more guilt for not having done what in fact was impossible for them to do at that stage of their development. The guilt is internalized to read, "I must be a bad person for this to have happened to me."

Some hard realities

- There is a flourishing market for kiddie porn in North America.
- In approximately 25 percent of child abuse cases, the victims are under the age of six.

- Within the family, sexual abuse is often initiated when the victim is four to six years old and continues until age eleven or beyond.
- In almost all reported cases, an abused child is subjected to sexual assault more than once.
- In roughly half of all cases, the offender is a person in a position of trust.
- On average, a career child molester will amass over sixty victims.
- Approximately 30 percent of sex offenders go on to commit further crimes.
- Many sex offenders have abused for fifteen years or more before they are discovered.
- Mentally and physically handicapped children are especially vulnerable to abuse.
- In a growing number of disclosures, children say they were subjected to sexual abuse during adult rituals.

These facts are not easy to write, read, or comprehend. How can we ever look at abusers with anything but anger? Who are they? How did they become so depraved, so evil?

Types of offenders
There are two basic types of offenders.

Pedophiles
Pedophiles are turned on by children. They buy kiddie porn magazines, choose careers or volunteer work that give them opportunities to have access to children, or haunt playgrounds. Some are serial abusers who use bribes and other means of coercion. They are often "good citizens." Some are married. Some exhibit no outward sign of inner disturbance. Some prey on

small boys who will, if undiscovered and uncounseled, grow up to become the next generation of abusers.

When a pedophile is discovered, public response often includes a cover-up, disbelief of the child's story, a focus on the child's sexual precocity, or a desire to help this valued member of the community who has had a "momentary slip." When an institution is involved, protection for it may also play a role. Protective reactions often free the abuser to continue the abuse, either at the same scene or in a new environment.

These men may feel like children themselves and prefer contact with those who are at a similar level of emotional growth, a level that may well have become fixated through their own childhood trauma of neglect, physical abuse, or, most commonly, sexual abuse. *Fixated offenders* believe that they can achieve affection only through victimizing a child. Equating sexuality with affection, many fixated offenders initiate and continue abuse without ever linking their own deep pain with the suffering and trauma they are causing. They see justification in what they do and feel little or no shame. They may marry just to have access to stepchildren or other young relatives.

Sometimes sexual abusers who are given in-depth training can learn the skills and methods necessary to control their deviant behavior. However, treatment for fixated pedophiles is seldom successful.

Family offenders

People in a caretaking role form another category of abusers. These include father, grandfather, stepfather, older cousin, uncle, family friend, babysitter, and other people in caretaking roles. They will often back down when faced with a firm "no" or with lack of cooperation on the child's part.

Many are themselves the victim of childhood abuse. These adults are emotionally unstable. Under stress — unemployment, marriage dysfunction, lack of a socially approved sexual outlet — they look to children for sympathy, affection, and recognition. They often choose children who are in awe of them, sometimes miniature replicas of people they love, and woo them with gifts, promises, and warmth. These men may feel great remorse if they are discovered and may be treatable.

Eighty-five percent of incest victims are female. Only one in forty biological fathers abuse their daughters, but one in six stepfathers abuse their stepdaughters. The abuse usually begins when the girl is between six and eleven. Incest occurs at all economic levels, within all ethnic groups, and in very "normal" families. The husband may be autocratic, the wife submissive, less educated, and financially and emotionally dependent on her husband. She herself may have been sexually abused as a child. The oldest daughter may take over running the family, including satisfying the father's sexual and emotional needs, especially in cases where the mother is ill, absent, alcoholic, or mentally ill. If an older daughter leaves or refuses to submit, the father may turn to a younger child. Some older girls have continued to submit to the father to protect younger siblings.

Children's responses

Many children silently endure abuse for long periods of time. How do they manage to survive?

Some make some kind of meaning out of the abuse: "It is okay for this to be happening to me because . . ." Others survive by splitting away from the hurting part of the self to become "another person" observing in a detached way — a mode of defense known as split personality syndrome. Multiple personalities, more common in women than men, were once thought bizarre manifestations of mental illness, but are now being recognized as a rather common response of children who have suffered abuse. A case has been reported of 23 different personalities housed inside the one body.

More aware children develop a deep and abiding sense of betrayal and of repressed rage at the abuser and the parent who doesn't protect. They feel acute loneliness; no one seems to care or want to listen when their need is so great to find someone who will help relieve the pain of being abused.

These children sit in our classrooms. Many are outwardly calm and come from what we presume are healthy families. But they do give out signals. Sometimes their hurting is evident below the calm; sometimes the signals are right up front for us to observe.

The following list, compiled from several sources, describes some of the symptoms. These symptoms do not necessarily indicate sexual abuse, of course, but any one could be an indicator of something amiss. Several symptoms together should be taken very seriously.

For instance, experts consider the following two indicators to be sure signs of sexual abuse, especially when they appear together:

- a host of physical complaints or problems (rashes, vomiting, headaches) that have no medical explanation
- sexual preoccupation (excessive or public masturbation and an unusual interest in sexual organs, sex play, and nudity)

We should also watch for students who:

- begin to decline academically
- show regressive behavior, for instance in toilet training
- spend more time alone than is customary
- become abusive or aggressive with teachers or other students
- daydream more often than usual
- cry more readily than usual
- "forget" gym clothes or refuse to change clothes in front of others
- produce artwork that includes sexually explicit details
- show evidence of eating and sleeping disturbances
- become angry and withdrawn
- show a lot of guilt, fear, or anxiety
- jump or pull away when touched
- show reluctance to go to a particular place with a particular person
- are fearful of bathrooms, showers, or closed doors
- are fearful of going home after school
- talk about running away from home or actually do so
- escape into fantasy
- become hyperactive
- have poor peer relationships

- show a massive weight change
- do things to destroy their appearance, including self-mutilation
- show a fear of males
- develop a pseudo-maturity
- act seductively
- experience abdominal pain
- have soreness, bleeding, swelling, or discharge in the vaginal area
- show sexual knowledge inappropriate for their age
- have torn, stained, or bloody clothing
- have difficulty walking or sitting
- become sexually promiscuous
- discuss suicide or attempt it
- become involved in drugs

The hints are there. Many children try, subconsciously, to disclose through one or more of the symptoms on this list. A few even tell, although often they are not believed. Evidence indicates, however, that we frequently do not pick up on their signals. Why not? And what can we do to change that?

What can we do?

Knowledge

Unfortunately, teachers receive only minimal training in recognizing child abuse, whether physical or sexual. Many hesitate to become involved because of their lack of knowledge, the lack of supportive resources in the school, or their own emotional discomfort. In fact, there are indications that some teachers feel considerable anxiety about society's expectations of them in this area.

Fortunately, more and more resources are becoming available all the time. For example, teachers in my school have access to a booklet, published by the Canadian Department of Justice, called *What to Do if a Child Tells You of Sexual Abuse*. Our school library also has a simple but effective picture book for children, *The Secret of the Silver Horse*, that stresses the need to tell when someone is doing something that hurts. *Feeling Yes, Feeling No* is a set of three National Film Board of Canada videos that, with its comprehensive teaching guide, provides excellent material for use in all grades.

Lack of knowledge and resources can be remedied, but teachers' personal discomfort may not be so easily overcome. Some teachers may have difficulty functioning in the student-teacher relationship with a child they know or suspect has been sexually abused. Some may choose not to show the videos, for instance, because they are uncomfortable with the topic, or because they are afraid a student might disclose abuse afterwards. Personal discomfort is an important factor when dealing with any emotional or values-laden issue and it must be respected. If you realize that is a factor for you, why not approach your administrator so that someone else, perhaps the librarian or the family studies teacher, can cover the material in your place?

Action

If you correctly read the signals from an abused child, or a child discloses abuse to you, what happens next? Some school boards have produced guides to help their teachers cope with either situation. One such guide, from the Hastings County School Board in Ontario, includes the following advice:

- Comments like these will invite children to disclose and provide them with an opportunity to confide in you: "I've noticed that you don't seem happy these days." "I'm worried about you — is anything wrong?" "Is there anything I can do to help?" "Would you like to talk to anyone else?"

- If children do disclose, reassure them that it was right to do so. Take the disclosure at face value. It's not your responsibility to debate accuracy, and, in any case, statistics indicate that children seldom lie about abusive situations.

- Regardless of the details given, don't allow your own judgment to show on your face or in the tone of your voice. Remain calm and supportive of the child's feelings.

- Never promise to keep a secret, even if the children ask you to. Reasonable doubt is enough to notify the principal, who in turn will ask the appropriate social service agency to investigate. Should your principal decide not to proceed and you feel it's imperative, notify the agency yourself. (In Canada, all teachers and other professionals are legally obliged to do so.)

Scars

For many children, disclosure brings incredible relief, especially if the abuser is arrested. Even if no charges are laid, the agency will protect the child by ordering the abuser to stay away or removing the child from the home. But there is no escape from the turmoil the whole family will experience. One or both parents will feel deep anger, fear, and guilt. Why did he/she/they not provide better protection for the child?

How could they have been so trusting of this person known to them? Parents have been known to minimize a child's story in order to salvage their own emotional stability or family ties. A woman I know continues to visit her grandfather for regular Sunday dinners. She still hates to hug him goodbye, though it has been years since her disclosure ended the abuse.

The victims become the center of family disruption, chaos, and emotional turmoil. They often feel totally at fault and burdened with guilt for contributing to the abuse by not resisting and not telling until now. Your support is critical at this point to help the children see that it was never their fault. Responsibility always lies with the adult.

If the abuser is charged, questions must be answered over and over again and to many people. Months drag on, with dates set and then changed. Testimony must be given in court. I will never forget the sight of two teenage girls leaving the courtroom after questioning by the man's defense lawyer. I saw their tears and watched them collapse into chairs after their ordeal.

Fortunately, the legal system has begun to recognize the terror children may feel in such trying circumstances, and some court appearances can now be videotaped privately and shown later. Shields are sometimes installed so the young person does not have to face the defendant. Still, I know of one girl who lives in constant fear of the day her abuser is released — will she have to see him on the street?

The degree to which children recover from sexual abuse depends on many factors. The closer the level of trust and the closer the relationship between abuser and victim, the greater the trauma. The longer the abuse continued, the longer and greater will be the impact. The extent of the abuse, the age of the child, the support of significant adults after disclosure are all factors affecting the child's ability to understand and eventually be healed.

Some children are survivors who can withstand a lot of pressure and go on with their lives. Others bury the abuse because they cannot function otherwise; these children can be devastated if and when memories surface later on. A depressed young woman told me that one day her memory was unlocked and she could see every detail again: the room, the curtains blowing at the window, the wallpaper, her father, and what he was doing. She was still experiencing the consequences, but at least now she knew the *why* of her bouts of sadness. Other survivors echo her sense of damage. Children who have suffered sexual abuse have experienced a horror unknown to most of us.

When these children feel most alone, believing they are the only ones ever to have experienced such things, they are filled with shame and guilt and they need our support as never before. Someone must be there for them. If our own emotional fragility or strong feelings do not permit us to become involved, then others must be found who can fill in. For there are indications that with the right kind of assistance and support, many of these wounded children will begin to integrate their experience and forget it. Or *seem* to forget it. Even with all the loving support we can give, however, the scars remain.

One-quarter of abused girls develop serious psychological problems with self-esteem, trust, and intimacy. As adults they are more anxious, depressed, and guilt-ridden than most women. Little boys who have been abused are likely to become the next generation of abusers, unless they are discovered and counseled. Abused girls grow up to marry men who will abuse them and their children: alcoholics, batterers, psychological and sexual abusers. They become rape victims; nearly two-thirds of women abused as children report being victims of rape or attempted rape. Sixty percent of teenage prostitutes were sexually abused as children; 47 percent have been raped. Poor self-image, lack of assertiveness, and the feeling that they deserve to be punished are all part of the pattern.

There are few women abusers. A few deeply damaged mothers may look to daughters to provide their sexual outlet or to a son to become a surrogate husband, but societal training has tended to keep women from becoming aggressive abusers.

As I came to the end of writing this chapter, I discovered that my outrage had changed to a feeling of helplessness. What can I possibly do, one teacher working in one school? Not much, perhaps, except to be aware and to act in a warm, caring manner when I recognize an abused child. What can you and I do together? Much more. Here are some ways you can join with me to help.

- Support your teachers' union or any group that works for the rights of children.
- Examine your own feelings about sexual abuse. What are your fears and concerns? How far are you able and willing to go to listen in a non-judgmental way, and to reach out with support for a hurting child?

- Create a climate in your classroom where children feel free to talk about anything. By revealing who you are and what you feel, you show your acceptance of them and your willingness to listen.
- Validate and honor the children's feelings and be understanding of the behavior that follows.
- Encourage girls to be assertive and outgoing. Advise them not to internalize their anger but to use positive ways of expressing it.
- Initiate or continue lessons on sexual abuse in every school year and encourage other staff members to do the same.
- Allow children to say "no" under certain circumstances.
- Work toward the elimination of pornography and violence against women through media literacy programs and the expression of your views.
- Begin at the primary grades to monitor the needy, clingy, low-esteem girls and the aggressive, bullying, angry boys. Find special programs to meet the emotional needs of these children.
- Look upon your classroom and school as a safe haven where children can find security in routine and in your acceptance of them as valued human beings.
- Learn about body language and behavioral messages that indicate hurt. Remember that an obnoxious child is a hurting child.
- And lastly, tune into your warm heart, your inner sense of how to deal with children who are in deep emotional pain. Be a friend. Be a person to be trusted when others are betraying them. Be there for them.

Sexual Abuse

Resources for Adults

A BETTER SAFE THAN SORRY BOOK: A FAMILY GUIDE FOR SEXUAL ASSAULT PREVENTION, Sol and Judith Gordon, Ed-U Press Inc., 1984.

GETTING STARTED: A RESOURCE MANUAL FOR GROWING A COMMUNITY BASED SEXUAL ABUSE TREATMENT PROGRAM IN YOUR COMMUNITY, Halton Sexual Abuse Program, Oakville, Ontario, 1991.

THE MOTHER'S BOOK, HOW TO SURVIVE THE MOLESTATION OF YOUR CHILD, Carolyn Byerly, Kendall Hunt Publishing Co., 1992.

SECRET SCARS: A GUIDE FOR SURVIVORS, Cynthia Crosson Tower, Viking/Penguin Books, 1989.

A VERY TOUCHING BOOK FOR LITTLE PEOPLE AND BIG PEOPLE, Jan Hindeman, AlexAndria, 1983.

WHEN CHILDREN INVITE CHILD ABUSE, Svea J. Gold, Fern Ridge Press, 1986.

WHAT TO DO IF A CHILD TELLS YOU OF SEXUAL ABUSE, Canadian Department of Justice, 1989.

NATIONAL CLEARINGHOUSE ON FAMILY VIOLENCE
Family Violence Prevention Division
Social Services Program Branch
Health & Welfare Canada
Ottawa, Ontario
K1A 1B5
1-800-267-1291

Resources for Children

EVERYTHING YOU NEED TO KNOW ABOUT INCEST, Karen Spies, Rosen Group, 1991.

IT HAPPENS TO BOYS TOO ... by Jane Satullo and Robert Russell, Berkshire Press, 1989.

IT'S NOT YOUR FAULT, Judy Jance, Franklin Press, 1985. (ages 4-9)

LOVING TOUCHES, Lory Freeman, Parenting Press, 1985. (ages 3-8)

NO MORE SECRETS FOR ME, Orelle Watcher, Little, Brown, 1986. (ages 3-7)

THE SECRET OF THE SILVER HORSE, Canadian Department of Justice, 1989.

SOMETHING HAPPENED AND I'M SCARED TO TELL: A BOOK FOR YOUNG CHILDREN VICTIMS OF ABUSE, Patricia Kehoe, Parenting Press, 1987.

Video

NATIONAL FILM BOARD OF CANADA (see Appendix for address)
FEELING YES, FEELING NO - A Sexual Assault Prevention Program for Young Children. A video with teaching guide to purchase or rent.

SERIOUS ILLNESS

*When her mom has an epileptic seizure, this grade three girl
no longer screams in terror, but calmly helps her older sister
get a blanket and care for their only parent.*

• • • • •

*When the father of a student suffered a severe stroke, I didn't
find out for a month. I kept asking about him and soon the
child said, "Please don't ask. When I want to, I'll tell you."
Humbled, I agreed. Every day thereafter I found a note on my
desk detailing the father's progress.*

• • • • •

*A grade eight boy wrote to me in his journal that today was
his non-custodial mother's birthday, and that it would be her
last, since she would be dead before the next one. He had
heard one side of a conversation and caught the word "cancer." We called his dad, who agreed to get more details. It
turned out that the doctor's examination had merely been
exploratory and at worst the boy's mom would have to
undergo a hysterectomy.*

• • • • •

*She had been in and out of doctors' offices for her back pains.
Before her appointment at the Hospital for Sick Children, I
asked this grade eight girl what she feared most.
"Being in a wheelchair," she said.*

• • • • •

Although most schools do not have large numbers of seriously ill students, perhaps no more than one in thirty, even one sick child affects the school community, as does any serious illness of the parents, grandparents, or other close relatives of the students. Children often lack specific information about their own illness or that of a loved one and so are not prepared to cope.

The question is whether we ourselves are prepared to cope with serious illness. When we need to help confused and frightened children, it is important that we begin by examining our own beliefs, attitudes, feelings, and, most importantly, our own fears about illness.

Do you remember any instance of serious illness in your own family when you were a child? My attitudes have certainly been shaped by my past experiences. When any of my own children wanted to stay home from school, I demanded proof of illness in fevers or spots. I almost never take sick days, because I tell myself I do not have time to be sick. I have little patience for sickness, especially if I think it is borderline.

Yet, as a small child, I watched my epileptic uncle fall to the floor in seizures. I saw my maternal grandfather, an Alberta coal miner, struggle for breath as a result of asthma and chronic bronchitis. My mother suffered from one illness after another.

I believe that I coped then by tucking my fears of illness and sick people deep into my unconscious. As a result, I became an adult who tried to repress and deny anxiety about illnesses. My sister did the same. When she first began to suffer from arthritis, she waited so long to go to a doctor that she needed an artificial hip almost immediately.

I have since learned how differently other people cope with illness. Some people answer the ubiquitous "How are you?" with streams of genuine and imaginary detail. Others are more matter-of-fact in describing medical problems. Some children need to see the school secretary or health nurse with the slightest ache. Others leave, without warning, for protracted hospital stays. Some relate what turn out to be false alarms. Some calmly describe actual instances of cancer or heart attacks or other serious threats to a loved one.

Seriously ill students

I once gave the opening address for a special workshop on ill children to an audience of educators, school nurses, home care workers, and parents. After my talk I stayed to learn and came away invigorated by everyone's obvious caring and concern. Parent Karen Anderson, whose eleven-year-old son Douglas had been fighting leukemia for two-and-a-half years, gave a moving plea for more awareness, knowledge, and preparation for children.

I decided then that it would not do for me to continue to "muddle through" the problems of serious illness. I knew I had a lot to learn about the topic, so I consulted others with more knowledge. I had one basic question for them all: "How can we help children who are ill and those who are dealing with the illness of a loved one?"

Here are samples of the answers I got.

- Norm Slater, a counselor at a nearby mental health clinic, and Neil Lamper, a retired professor of psychology and a therapist, both said, "Listen to the children. They'll tell you what they need and want."

- Marilyn McIntosh, school board social worker, said, "When I was three my brother was diagnosed as diabetic. Someone gave me a coloring book. Don't forget the needs of the siblings."

- My two school administrators both stressed the need for communication between home and school. The son of one had experienced serious illness, the son of the other an accident. They both mentioned how much it meant to them, as parents, when they received a call from their sons' teachers. Unfortunately, my principal estimates that only about 25 percent of teachers feel confident and comfortable enough to phone a sick child's home to ask about his or her illness.

It soon became apparent that establishing clear, supportive, ongoing communication is vital — with students, parents, siblings, classmates, and others who deal with the child. For instance, the whole staff — gym teachers, custodians, bus drivers, yard supervisors, secretaries — need to know some things, like what limitations an arthritic child has, what we need to watch for in a diabetic child, or what kindnesses are due to a returning-from-hospital child.

Most of us respond with care and concern to the seriously ill students in our classrooms. We are conscientious about sending homework home and about modifying the curriculum and our expectations of the children. I cannot imagine anyone writing on a child's report: "He must attend school more regularly to succeed" if that child's absences result from regular hospital visits for dialysis. Most of us try to provide extra assistance when inevitable absences create great gaps in understanding in the formal school curriculum. We arrange for class letters and cards to be sent to the hospital or to the child's home. Many visit or call, and encourage the other students to keep in touch with their absent classmates. We are mindful of the physical limitations of ill students in the classroom, making sure they have the correct physical setting and the support of friends when they need it. We watch out for cruel peers who tease and act hurtfully or carelessly around sick students.

But there are some things many of us do not do. In particular, not enough of us make it our business to learn all we can about the illnesses of our students. We rely on hazy general knowledge when the school nurse might have readily available information to share with us. In fact, we should keep in touch with the nurse on a regular basis so we know what specific information is going to and coming from the parents.

The need for information

As the very helpful book *Crisis Counseling with Children* points out, "At some time we all encounter children who are very ill. How do you explain heart disease to a five-year-old? What do you say to the teenage girl who is balding and overweight, side effects from the chemotherapy for cancer? Or how do you respond to the stricken faces in your group of ten-year-olds when one of them is having a seizure?"

I was curious about the level of understanding children have about various illnesses, so I surveyed a grade eight class. I asked them to tell me, anonymously, what they thought happened to a person's body as a result of certain diseases or conditions. I found that the percentage of students who had at least a basic understanding of some common illnesses was surprisingly small: AIDS 36 percent (and I had taught a unit on it the year before!), Alzheimer's disease 43 percent, arthritis 57 percent, diabetes 50 percent (there was a diabetic in the other grade eight class), asthma 81 percent (because it is common?), epilepsy 50 percent, strokes 29 percent, heart attacks 43 percent, multiple sclerosis 29 percent, and cancer 29 percent. Nor did they do well in a later survey regarding the causes of cancer and its prevalence — urgent information since today approximately one in three North Americans develops cancer.

Most students have a lot of misinformation, misconceptions, and fears about illness. We need to understand that when serious illness strikes children personally, they often:

- use their imaginations to weave their own sense (perhaps unrealistically and unnecessarily negative) out of the bits and pieces they hear and out of the body language and tension they experience around them

- hold in or cover up their own feelings and questions to protect the adults whose concerns and fears they recognize
- feel guilty because they think the illness is their fault — the little ones especially may believe that they caused the problem or that they must have done something bad to deserve this punishment
- are afraid and therefore angry — at the healthy world, at their own powerlessness, at their God — and take their anger out on those who are trying to help them: nurses and doctors, parents, teachers, and other students

We need to have as many accurate facts about their illnesses as we can gather, and we need to talk with the children truthfully. They will process as much information as they are developmentally able to, in the same way as they process information about sex. That is why the little ones may ask the same questions over and over. It is only fair to tell them whatever truth they can handle, but judging what they can handle may prove tricky. In general, I've found that they can handle more than we give them credit for.

On the other hand, some sick children and their families are subject to information overload. Bits and pieces of information come at them from all sides until they feel confused, exhausted, and exasperated, and some doctors will not (or cannot) communicate clearly enough to help them understand. Should we bother these parents with our phone calls of inquiry? Yes. Karen Anderson pointed out that there is never a bad time to call. The thoughtfulness behind the call will be appreciated even if the parent responds with a harried or shaky tone.

The fears and the hope

Author Erma Bombeck wrote a wonderful book on children and cancer called *I Want to Grow Hair, I Want to Grow Up, I Want to Go to Boise.* She tried very hard to begin with a tone that was upbeat and even funny, but when she read a draft of the first chapter to a group of young cancer patients, they told her she had to start with the most important question and title the chapter: "Am I Gonna Die?"

That is not the only fear cancer patients and children with other serious illnesses have, however. They are also afraid of being incapacitated, of being in a wheelchair, of being mutilated or becoming blind, of pain, of pills, of loss of hair, of being different, of being teased, of falling behind in school work, of missing out on sports, dances, Halloween and other special times, of losing friends. Small children fear strange new places, new people, and, especially, the times when their mommy or daddy can't be there.

And yet sick children want to be treated the same as anybody else. A cancer patient told Bombeck: "I had a teacher last year who shouted at me on the first day of school, 'Sit down and be quiet!' She treated me like everyone else. I knew it was going to be a good year." That teacher knew what she was doing. Sick children, and those grieving for sick loved ones, need the security of knowing their teachers are in control. From us they want warmth, tolerance, and acceptance. They, in turn, will teach us about courage, humor under stress, and hope.

Even so, it may at times be up to us to dispense the hope. A diabetic student once had a very difficult time following hospitalization for a serious coma. It was I who had to say to her: "I don't believe the diagnosis you were given that you'll be dead by the age of twenty-four. You're a fighter. You've been a fighter for as long as I've known you. The advances in diabetes research are wonderful and will continue to happen. You are going to come through this door fifteen years from now and tell me all about your wonderful life as the lawyer you are going to become. Not for one minute do I believe otherwise."

Siblings are vulnerable too

If a sick child has siblings in the same class, or elsewhere in the school, it is important to remember Marilyn McIntosh's advice to keep their needs in mind. Siblings, too, are likely to suffer and in similar ways.

They will fear for the welfare of their ill brother or sister, and they may lash out in anger or suffer feelings of guilt. "Why am I upset by all the attention he's getting? How can I be so selfish? I'm jealous when he is pampered and gets so many treats while I'm shipped off to relatives or friends. I feel unimportant and unloved. But I'm healthy, so I should be grateful and feel sorry for him instead."

These children suffer anxiety and isolation. They observe parental worry and feel unable to help. They may have periods of depression, behavioral and sleep problems, or fears about their own health. Sometimes they manifest physical symptoms of the same disease in order to get the same kind of attention. Unfortunately, their feelings are often ignored, both at home and in school. We need to remember that they, too, need someone to listen to them, validate their feelings, and offer reassurance.

The sick child's classroom

Fear and anger also threaten a sick child's classroom. A classroom is like a family in some respects; when one member experiences stress, all are affected. We need more class discussion about sick students and their illnesses to provide facts and validate feelings. Peers need to understand that sick children are often cranky and difficult. I like to arrange for discussions before the return of a temporarily absent student, especially about the kind of support that child may need.

Sick parents

Earlier I mentioned a girl whose father had been in the intensive care unit for a whole month after a stroke before I was told. In line with her family's code, she had kept it a secret from all but a few friends. One day I tried to talk to her younger sister about her father's illness, but got only a bare minimum of details. Yet her body clearly communicated her feelings as she silently brushed away the tears.

Deep and forceful feelings are a natural part of the life of a child who has a very sick parent. On this topic I learned much from Eda LeShan's book *When a Parent Is Very Sick.*

On hearing that a parent is seriously ill, a child's first emotion is disbelief, followed by feelings of fear, guilt, anger, and helplessness. Younger children believe in the magical omnipotence of parents — those powerful adults who can be counted on to take care of them and keep them safe from harm. Their minds are filled with questions: Will my father die? What did I do to make him sick? Who will take care of me? Is this catching? Might I also get sick and die? One child sat up all night, listening through a glass pressed against the closet wall between her room and the bedroom of her parents. Her mother was ill and no one was talking to her about it.

As teachers, we need to watch for symptoms of shock, fear, and guilt. And even more important, we need to accept the child's anger, which is a natural part of the process. We have to accept that feelings are neither good nor bad — they just are. "How can my mother do this to me?" or "How could my father be so careless as to get sick when I need him?" a child might wail inwardly, followed by a guilty: "I must be a terrible person to be thinking like this."

Adults may make these negative emotions worse by trying to shield children from the truth, in the mistaken belief that they are protecting them. But if they do not know, many students imagine the situation to be far worse than it really is. What does "hysterectomy" mean to a nine-year-old? What exactly is a stroke? Telling children the truth about an illness and involving them in coping with it is the best way of helping them deal with the changes in their lives.

And there will be many changes, particularly at home. Their lives will be filled with confusion, impatience, and stress. They may have to deal with embarrassment, or even repugnance, as a beloved parent changes, perhaps becomes ravaged by illness. Time and attention will be lost to them as the parents cope with hospitalization or extended home care and with each other's emotional needs. An only child may suffer great loneliness; an oldest child may be given too much responsibility; a younger child may become a scapegoat, a dumping ground for the negative feelings of the rest of the family. Siblings will sometimes draw together for comfort, but they can also become each other's targets for tension-releasing bullying and teasing.

Most seriously ill parents recover, but strangely enough, their recovery can also produce negative feelings. There is relief, of course, but also disappointment. The parent, the object of such worry and concern, returns to normal and not sainthood. Longstanding tensions between parent and child resurface. A different type of anger may appear in the child: "How could you have worried me so much?" Routines and special privileges set up during the illness disappear. When things are safe again, the pain and anger that were submerged during the illness can be released.

What can we do?

Changed behavior may be the first clue we get. Children who are ill, or children of ill parents, may not tell you anything directly. In fact, they may have been told little or nothing themselves. But you may sense uneasiness, withdrawal, sudden changes in their learning habits, dark circles under their eyes, sadness, or listlessness. Look also for acting out, stealing, or clinging.

When you notice any of these behaviors, a private conversation is in order: "I think something is troubling you. I'd like to listen and help if you'd like to share with me. Now or whenever, I'll be available." Many children will remain reticent and you may learn little about the situation. But, more than anything, these children need an adult supporter, someone to confide in, someone to answer questions that no one else has time for; someone to give reassurances that, no matter what, they will not be left without people who will love and care for them.

Point out to these children that grown-ups often becoming cranky because of worry and fear. Reassure them by explaining that although their own emotions will be very unsteady for a while, one day everything will settle down into a pattern. Tell them that being brave is hard work, and give them a retreat to go to if their feelings overwhelm them during class. Encourage them to write their feelings in a journal or in creative writing, or in notes and letters to the sick parent or sibling. Painting, drawing, running, or another physical activity can lift sadness, anger, and grief, as well.

I am fortunate in having access to an office where students can come regularly for private talks, and I am always there well before class time. Some days students just pass by to say, "No change"; other days they need more time with me. Children connected with illness need our sustained caring and concern and the stability of day-to-day routines. When everything else changes so drastically, the classroom and the school remain constant. There is much solace in this.

Parents also need to know that everything is under control. You may want to set up an interview with the healthy parent, or with one or both parents in the case of children who are demonstrating that they are not coping well with their own illness or that of a sibling. Explain what has been happening in class, and what kind of support their children are receiving. Reassure them that the curriculum will be covered as well as it can be under the circumstances and that a lot of kindness will fill up any curriculum gaps.

Serious Illness

COME SIT BY ME, Heather Collins, Margaret Merrifield, Women's Press, 1990. Classroom and community reaction to a young boy, diagnosed HIV Positive. Sensitive and moving. (ages 6-9)

I WANT TO GROW HAIR, I WANT TO GROW UP, I WANT TO GO TO BOISE, Erma Bombeck, Harper Collins, 1990.

VANISHING COOKIES: DOING OK WHEN A PARENT HAS CANCER, Dr. Michelle Goodman, Benjamin Family Foundation, 1990.

WHEN A PARENT IS VERY SICK, Eda LeShan, Little, Brown, 1986.

ABLELINK
An open forum where disabled, isolated, and "abled" users of all ages discuss ideas and opinions across Canada.
Contact: Remote Data Systems, 919 Alness St., North York, Ontario, M3J 2J1. (416)650-6207, FAX (416)650-5073

SUDDEN DEATH

A young girl's father went to a chiropractor complaining of chest pains. Three weeks later he died of cancer.

• • • • •

A father with several children in our school was killed in a tragic car accident.

• • • • •

When a six-year-old child was killed, it looked like an accident. But later a thirteen-year-old was tried and convicted of murder.

• • • • •

A popular grade five student was killed one spring afternoon when the car in which he was a passenger left the road.

• • • • •

A train roared into a teacher's car as it crossed a railway track, and her primary class had to be told the news when they arrived at school the next morning.

• • • • •

The school is rocked and shocked. Rumors fly. Staff and students look at each other with stunned faces. Emotions range from blankness to hysteria. A death has occurred — a student or parent or teacher has died. It cannot be ignored. What do you do during those first awful hours and days?

Our own response

What has your experience been with death? What is your comfort level with the topic? We live in a society that worships youth and activity and pretends we are all immortal. Gone are the days of black armbands, wreaths on doors, and a year of formal mourning. Few of us talk easily about death. We buy suitable cards instead.

When my much loved, gentle father died, I took my cue from the way my mother and sister coped, and cried only when I saw him in his casket. But grief subsequently turned my strong mother into a shell of a person. Her own death was a relief from the pain of severe arthritis but, again, only a few tears were shed by those of us who survived her. I went through the first stages of open grieving, but soon stopped myself and did what most of us tend to do: "Get on with it, put it behind you, carry on." People were stoic at my sister's funeral as well. When one friend broke down and wept, she apologized, but maybe she was the only one being honest about her feelings.

"How is she?" is the usual question about a woman who has lost a husband. "She's taking it well" is the usual reply, meaning that she's not embarrassing us with outward grieving. Men, of course, are not expected to show any emotion at all. But John Bradshaw believes that if you have not gone through extended periods of anger, remorse, hurt, depression, sadness, and loneliness, you have not done your "grief work." The energy that is blocked will rise again, especially when you face a subsequent loss. It may emerge, for instance, when a sudden death hits your school community.

We teachers are having to play an increasingly crucial support role for children faced with death, because they have less and less access to trained religious leaders and wise elders in the community. We need to prepare for that role.

In the past I may have been insensitive to signals my students have given. I sometimes provided appropriate picture books or had (unproductive) talks with hurting children, but I could not cope with their real needs because of my personal ignorance and discomfort. However, I have come to recognize how important it is, in helping students deal with death, to be personally strong and stable — which means that teachers who may still be fragile on this topic themselves must receive consideration and assistance from others in the school community.

We also need to know what to expect. What is death like for children? As adults do, children go through any or all of the following stages:

- Shock: "I can't believe it!"
- Denial: "I won't believe it!"
- Bargaining: "I'll do anything to bring him or her back!"
- Anger: "It can't be happening!"
- Depression: "It is happening and I can't bear it!"

Finally, two to five years later, they get to healing and acceptance: "It has happened and I have grieved enough to go on!"

Knowing something about these stages may help you give some direction to those who are experiencing them. People around you, including parents, will appreciate your sensitivity and knowledge.

How children perceive and react to death

Children will respond to the experience of death in different ways.

Birth to 5

Under the age of five, children cannot conceive of the finality of death, nor can they understand that it could happen to them. They believe the dead person will revive, or is eating, dressing, and functioning in some other place. They'll ask if there's a McDonald's there, or TV, and if the person will be playing or working. Television reinforces the idea of reviving or relocating, since cartoon characters regularly get flattened, then pop back to life. Characters die in one show and come back into robust life in the next.

However, young children are deeply affected and adept at picking up body language cues that indicate adult stress. Adults may find children's behavior inappropriate and disrespectful; they may repeat the same annoying questions, ask to touch the corpse, make irrelevant observations, ask for a new daddy, mommy, brother, sister, aunt. These children are simply asking for reassurance in their own way. Experts stress the need for acceptance of these responses. There is no such thing as a wrong or bad response, unless it is physically harmful to themselves or others.

Little ones live in the age of magic. Between the ages of three and six, children often believe that their thoughts and actions had a direct link with the death

— if only they had gone to bed on time or had not been rude to the dead person. . . . . Young children need to be told at the outset, and frequently, that the death was not their fault. Unfortunately, many adults in an early stage of their own grieving do not respond appropriately to children's confusion and fears.

Six to 12

Older children more easily accept their own mortality and see death as irreversible. They often view death as something personified, as an evil, mysterious and scary monster, a skeletal figure, or a ghost. While kindergarten and preschool teachers may be puzzled by the bizarre talk and behavior of their students, primary and junior teachers may wonder why theirs seem so little affected. For many children this age, denial is the primary defense and they carry on as if nothing has happened. Others become hyperactive, even hysterical. For too long in my teaching career I did not understand that hyperactivity in children often masks anxiety. As educators and caring adults, we must take it as a given that these children have been dreadfully hurt. The world will never again be an altogether safe and secure place.

As with serious illness, children this age often suffer intensely from guilt, especially over the death of a brother or sister with whom they had a difficult relationship.

Adolescents

Adolescents spend most of their energy trying to make sense of who they are in the world and who they will become. They are often confused, moody, egocentric, and needy. Death will come to them as a shocking, totally unfair destroyer. Traumatized teens can become very angry people, lashing out in all directions or turning inward toward depression. Some may begin to use body-destroying chemicals or take up other self-destructive habits.

Teenagers have a desperate need to be heard. They often feel judged, ignored, and unaccepted in the family grieving pattern. They long for compassion and understanding, yet hate being watched over by peers and adults. They are told they have to be strong when they feel like breaking down in front of the world. If they have no one to talk to, they can carry a great weight.

One girl who lost her father hated the fact that some of the other girls were "different" with her. I arranged several all-girl meetings where she openly told her classmates how angry she was at them, and where they explained that they could not understand that she was not showing more sadness. Together they (and I) learned a lot about grieving.

Another student, a boy who also lost his father, supported his grief-stricken mother by acting as if he, the only son, was now the man of the house. He did not come to me on his own, but when I invited him into my office he was very open about his feelings. My message to him was that he was still a child and, while he would miss his father for a long time, he could not become the father of the house.

Both students told me that they appreciated the condolences of their peers and the staff members, but that afterward they wanted to be treated the same as they had always been treated.

Listen and watch

For all these children, symptoms of distress become clear if we are aware and sensitive. Younger ones will not verbalize a lot of what they are feeling, but their behavior will give us strong messages. Thumb-sucking and other regressive behaviors may appear. Stomach-aches, sleeplessness, bedtime fears, and frequent clinging are common. Because children do not sustain grief the way adults do, they will be subject to periods of normal behavior followed by a plunge into one of the stages of grief. They may be playing, working, doing whatever kids do and then drop right back into anger or sadness.

Anniversaries are likely to be difficult, as are holidays and other special occasions, especially during the first year. Watch for extreme fragility when another loved one is threatened in some way. The day one grade six student found out that his grandfather had been taken to the hospital with a heart attack, he beat up a peer on the playground. He had lost his mother the year before. I gave him a basketball and sent him outside to bash it against a blank wall for as long as he liked. It helped.

Grieving often takes a long time, up to a lifetime for some. The more children are allowed to express their feelings and fears, the sooner they will recover. Children over the age of eight often wear a mask and give an overall message of control, saying in effect: "I'm perfectly okay and don't you dare treat me any differently." Unfortunately, many adults accept this overt behavior with a sense of relief: "Good! My child is handling this just fine. Let's carry on with life now." But repression is harmful. Some people believe it is not the trauma we suffer in childhood that causes later emotional illness, but the inability to express the trauma at the time. Children need to have someone in their lives who will tell them it is okay to feel whatever they are feeling and will give them strategies to deal with their emotions.

Perhaps doing a curriculum unit on death will help, as daunting as that may seem. I recently discussed death with a class of grade eight students and they were fascinated. Perhaps we should arrange for a funeral director to come for Career Week or take classes on a field trip to a funeral parlour. It is not unusual for students to visit a graveyard in search of pioneer information, but why not discuss current embalming practices and funeral arrangements with them? Death used to be much more present and visible. People died at home, the body was kept there, and the community mourned together. I was surprised to discover that eighty years ago approximately 65 percent of children under fifteen died, while today only 3 percent do. Today about 90 percent of people die in hospital and are immediately whisked away to a funeral home.

On the other hand, more and more of today's children experience the death of grandparents and, often, great-grandparents. A student learned of a loved great-grandfather's death early one morning. Midway through the first period, she put her head down on her desk and began to sob. The teacher sent her to me and we did some grieving work together. We talked about the hurt she was feeling. We read a book together to prepare her for the wake and funeral. She told me what he had been like and what she would miss about him. I gave her permission to stay in the library as long as she liked to look at magazines or photograph albums or just to think. After recess, she chose to go back and was able to carry on.

Events like this provide "teachable moments" when you can put regular work aside and gather the class for a discussion about death, for a sharing of how others coped and felt in similar circumstances. Do not hesitate to share your own anxieties and fears around death. When we adults show our feelings, we give children permission to do so as well.

Seeing a body in a casket will leave a lasting image for many children. They attend a wake or visit a funeral home where they see the corpse, and then can't get the image to leave — they close their eyes and it is there, or it appears in the midst of some unrelated activity. They are relieved when I tell them that it will gradually fade away. One girl almost freaked out at the funeral because she was sure her grandfather was breathing. At the graveside she had an urge to yell that he was not dead, but she contained herself. Had she not felt able to share this experience with me, she might have internalized and held that fear for the rest of her life.

Some children dream of the deceased. One girl kept dreaming of her grandmother hooked up to tubes in the hospital, the way she had last seen her. I suggested that she say each night before going to sleep: "Grandma, I know you loved me and wouldn't hurt me. It's okay if you come to me tonight." I also suggested that this girl and her younger sister write letters of farewell to their grandmother. If children have not had a chance to say a final goodbye, such a letter can ease their distress. One funeral home grief counselor had a student write a farewell letter to be put into the casket. Writing about the deceased in a poem or story is also good therapy. I have had poems handed in with accompanying tears and I am always supportive. It is good to cry. Tears are healing.

Given that not much comfort, assurance or information from distraught relatives at home may be available, and that death is almost a taboo subject in many parts of our culture, what is the responsibility of the school? Is dealing with death a maybe, a should, or a must? Surely the answer must arise out of our compassion for the emotional needs of our students.

The death of a student

How can the school deal with the death of a student? The very first step should be gathering the staff together. If it is apparent that one or more teachers cannot deal with the situation, arrangements need to be made for the principal, guidance teacher, school nurse, another staff member, or a substitute to take over. The children need strong adult support at this time.

Next, plan together how you will present factual information to the students. Rumors inevitably spring up, and they must be replaced by truth, as much of it as is known and as much as the children can benefit from knowing. Arrange for the announcement to be made in a calm, sensitive way. Options are the public address system or an assembly of the whole school, but I prefer to have teachers tell their own students, if possible.

You may want to suspend regular classes and plans, at least for the first part of the day. When a grade five child had been killed the afternoon before in a car accident, the class spent the time before morning recess outside with the teacher and principal, absorbing the facts individually and talking in small groups.

It is very important that the children be told, right at the outset, that any feelings that emerge are okay. If they are feeling sad and want to cry (and many will), you have to have lots of tissues. They may feel nothing. Their feelings may keep changing. They may feel angry. They may feel anxious, their stomachs doing flip-flops. They may feel the need to be silly. They may feel tired. All of this is acceptable and normal.

If you are substituting for another teacher and do not know the class intimately, reading aloud *I Had a Friend Named Peter* by Janace Cohn is a good beginning. Afterward ask the children to tell you about their classmate. What did he like to do best? What did he look like? What was she good at? Who were her special friends? The children will begin to share incidents, good memories, and bad ones. If someone remembers being unkind, calling the dead person a name, or bossing him or her around the day before, feelings of guilt can be acknowledged as normal and relieving.

Share how you feel inside and how sad you are about this tragedy. Allow the children to ask questions, answering as best you can the ones that touch on faiths, beliefs, and practices not your own. "I don't know" is always honest. Death is a great mystery and I encourage talk about it by asking: "Where do you think your classmate is now?" Most will mention Heaven or a similar final resting place. Many children have fears around the Higher Power of their faith (or non-faith) and it is important to suggest that the place where their classmate is will most likely be very beautiful and peaceful. Where are such places here on earth?

When I sense fear, I ask them whether they were afraid before they were born. I suggest that, whatever kind of afterlife there might be (or even if there is no afterlife, as some may believe), it will not be any more fearful than that.

After sharing a book and some conversation, most students will appreciate a return to regular classroom routines. Attention may be fragile, but there is solace in predictability when fear has entered their world.

What should you do with the desk and other physical belongings of the child now gone? It is cruel to whisk them away. Give the children an opportunity, that day or shortly after, to write a goodbye letter to their friend or the parent(s), recording something special and memorable about the dead child and specific things about him or her that will be missed. Encourage them to write what is in their hearts — and do the same yourself. At the end of the day, invite all those involved with the class (principal, other teachers, even secretaries) to gather around the desk, lay their letters on it and give a verbal goodbye as they leave. After school, the desk and belongings can be removed or changed and the letters delivered to the family.

I also make sure that a picture of the dead child is placed in a prominent place in the classroom for the rest of the school year, and I mention the child often. Grieving students have told me how much they appreciate sometimes hearing the name of the friend they miss so much. When no one talks about the dead, it is as if they never existed and, for children, that is hurtful.

Questions will arise almost immediately about possible attendance at the wake or funeral, and about donations or flowers from the school to the family. Sending something is much easier than attending, and some teachers just cannot face the gatherings. Yet it means a lot to the survivors to have a strong school delegation, so those who can should make the effort.

As for the children, sometimes it is appropriate to send the whole class to the wake or funeral, sometimes a delegation can be organized, and sometimes individual parents will decide. So much depends on the age of the students. Any children who attend should be carefully prepared for the experience. Using books, personal sharing, or simple explanations, you will want to discuss the process in detail: what kind of place it will be, what it may look like, what other people will be doing, and what will be expected of them. Most people will be visibly sad, and they may feel sad too. If possible, make yourself available afterward in case they want to talk about the experience.

Some classes or schools decide to create a memorial and involve the family in choosing a tree to plant during a special ceremony or in setting up a scholarship or award. This kind of activity can be a good step in the healing process.

The death of a teacher

Most of what I've said about the death of a student also applies to the death of a teacher.

The whole school needs to be involved in this event. Someone known to all the students should address them as soon as possible. Classroom talk about death is essential. Farewell letters, clearing the teacher's desk, and attendance at the ceremonies should receive similar attention. The teacher's picture should remain in a prominent place and every effort should be made to find a replacement who is caring, sensitive, and knowledgeable. The rest of the school year must be a time of gentle and respectful guidance and support.

The death of a parent

Concerns surrounding the death of a parent are somewhat different. In our school, a donation is sent and a representative delegation goes to the funeral home and the funeral. The school set up a memorial fund to assist one young widow financially. Because children who have lost a parent do not usually return to school until all the formalities and family functions are over, the class has time to decide how to show their condolences and, more importantly, how to act when the student returns.

Classmates often experience deep fears regarding their own mortality and that of their parents. One young girl who had little contact with her non-custodial parent became visibly upset at the death of a friend's father: What if her own daddy died and she didn't know? In the case of multiple deaths (after an accident or fire, for instance), the need for strong support is even more urgent. As before, rumors must be dealt with and the truth given.

With older classes, there is often great anxiety about how best to relay regrets and how to act when bereaved classmates return. I explain that their friends are the same people they knew before. Perhaps they will look and act sad, be more quiet, not show any emotion, or look and act the same as they always did. I may suggest that we all write letters to say what is in our hearts and deliver them ahead of time. I know from experience how much such letters are appreciated. They also make it unnecessary for the children to say anything more when their classmate returns.

Even so, returning to school is difficult for children. Above all, most hate the stares. It helps to explain that their peers stare for two reasons: they are curious about how they themselves would act in similar circumstances, and they wonder what it is like to have lost a parent. The fear of abandonment is one all children share.

What to watch for afterward

With all children, especially those who seem to be unaffected, we must continue to watch for signs of distress. Be especially aware of their fears concerning the remaining parent. One boy who had lost his father some years earlier pronounced himself unworried when his mother was in the hospital, but I noticed that he began to carry his father's picture around with him. After the death of a sibling, reactions may be both delayed and prolonged. Be alert to the effects of a subsequent move, the loss of a friend, and anniversaries. Use the death of a pet or a public figure to talk openly about the fact of death, so the issues can be raised and positive attitudes promoted in a non-threatening way.

Watch for symptoms that show a stopped-up grief process: learning difficulties that are new, unusual trouble-making, fatigue, or withdrawal. Watch for anger and offer strategies to deal with it. Alert the health nurse and/or principal when you suspect the child needs further assistance. Above all, listen, listen, listen. Allow a quiet child to communicate through a journal. Let formal curriculum go when necessary. Be very gentle in your marking for the next while. Be a stable influence in the life of the hurting child.

One summer, just before I left for my summer holiday, I heard that the single father of three of our students was dying of cancer. I left stamped, self-addressed envelopes with two staff members so I could be told if he died before September, and I made sure to take along the address of those students. A letter would be little comfort, I knew, but it was all I would be able to do from so far away. And even such small indications of caring are appreciated.

Look for programs or people to help you. But, even with help, there is no easy way to deal with death. Fortunately, we can take comfort in the knowledge that our care and concern can make the emotional load just a bit lighter for our students, fellow staff members, and parents.

Sudden Death

Resources for Adults

ON CHILDREN AND DEATH, Elizabeth Kubler-Ross, MacMillan, 1985.

A SEASON OF GRIEF: HELPING CHILDREN GROW THROUGH LOSS, Donna Gaffney, Plume, 1989.

HEALING THE SHAME THAT BINDS YOU, John Bradshaw, Health Communications, 1988.

HELPING CHILDREN COPE WITH SEPARATION AND LOSS, Claudia Jewett, Harvard Common Press, 1982.

RAINBOWS FOR ALL GOD'S CHILDREN, INC.
Support for the death or divorce of a parent (throughout North America).
1111 Tower Rd.
Schaumburg, IL 60173
708-310-1880

Resources for Children

ABOUT DYING, Sara B. Stein, Walker, 1984. (preschool-8)

THE FALL OF FREDDIE THE LEAF, Leo Buscaglia, Holt, Rinehart & Winston, 1982.

I HAD A FRIEND NAMED PETER: TALKING TO CHILDREN ABOUT THE DEATH OF A FRIEND, Janice Cohn, Morrow, 1987. (ages 5-9)

HOW IT FEELS WHEN A PARENT DIES, Jill Krementz, Knopf, 1988. (ages 5-10)

SUICIDE

They missed the school bus, so the grade twelve boy offered to drive his younger brother in the truck. He turned onto a road that led to a deep quarry and said he was going over the edge — would the brother come with him? Just before the truck hit the cliff, the younger boy jumped out.
The truck fell twenty meters.

• • • • •

His parents were out. He taped his suicide and later they heard him saying, "You aren't going to do this — you're too chicken." The tape ended with a gunshot.

• • • • •

She wakened her younger sister in the middle of the night, blood spurting everywhere from slit wrists. The younger child kept talking until her sister fell asleep, then spilled the story out to her teacher the next morning.

• • • • •

Returning from a party, the parents found their house locked. When the father broke in, he found his teenage son on their bed, dead from a gunshot wound.

• • • • •

In the last few years, suicide by children has become a significant topic of conversation and discussion in the media: on radio and TV; in newspapers and magazines; and in songs, artwork, and photographs. Children as young as three or four may pick up the word, and we should be aware that suicide is a real option even for younger children. However, there is still little published research about preteen suicide, and most of what follows refers to older students.

Most teachers know about one or more young people who have ended their lives. I remember a recent graduate who was serving a jail sentence. He had been allowed to spend Christmas at home, and he dreaded going back so much that he shot himself on Boxing Day while the rest of his family was out. Each time I hear about a student suicide, I hope it will be the last, but I know that is not likely.

At the end of one workshop I gave, a teacher told me how her daughter's ex-boyfriend was sitting talking to her in her living room when he took out a pistol and, before she could move, shot himself in the head. Another young high school boy killed himself in his ex-girlfriend's driveway. Still another took a shotgun up to a quarry; two much younger boys heard the shot and watched the boy die. Boys tend to use guns, ropes, and jumping from high places and, when they set out to end their lives, they usually succeed. Girls use barbituates and slash their wrists, but they often tell someone and do not succeed.

Statistics for the province of Ontario provide a good sample, although in some areas of North America they may be significantly higher or lower. For 1989, the coroner's office reported nineteen male and six female suicides in the ten — fourteen age group, and 218 male and twenty-nine female suicides in the fifteen — nineteen age group — more than five each week! Suicide is one of the leading causes of death among young people in both Canada and the United States, and for every successful suicide, fifty to 100 teens make attempts. We must also keep in mind that many suicide deaths are covered up by doctors concerned for the family, and others are deemed accidental, especially car accidents and drownings. Family, teachers, and friends are always left with these big questions: Why did it happen? What didn't we see? How could we have prevented this terrible waste?

You might want to test your level of knowledge and understanding of this growing and tragic phenomenon by guessing whether the following statements are true or false.

1   People who talk about suicide don't do it.
2. Suicide attempts happen without warning.
3. More women commit suicide than men.
4. Suicidal people are fully intent on dying.
5. Once a person is suicidal, he or she is suicidal forever.
6. Discussing suicide encourages people to do it.
7. Improvement following a suicidal crisis means that the risk is over.
8. Suicide happens more among the poor than among the rich.
9. Suicide runs in families.
10. All suicidal individuals are mentally ill.

Did you guess that all these statements are false? Here are the answers I found.

1. Of any ten persons who kill themselves, eight have talked about it beforehand.

2. Suicidal persons provide many advance clues and warnings.
3. Three times more women attempt suicide, but three times more men are successful.
4. Most suicidal people are undecided about living or dying. They gamble with death, leaving it to others to save them.
5. Individuals who think about killing themselves are truly "suicidal" for only a limited period of time.
6. Research shows that nearly all teenagers have thought about suicide at some time in their lives, whether or not anyone has talked about it to them. If they are thinking about it, then it is important for them to talk about it.
7. When other people think the problem is over, they start to pay less attention to the possibility. In fact, most suicides occur within about three months of the beginning of "improvement," when feelings are still raw and improvement is a day-to-day struggle.
8. Suicide is neither the disease of the rich nor a curse of the poor. It is very democratic.
9. Suicide does not run in families. It is an individual pattern.
10. Although suicidal persons are very unhappy, they are not necessarily mentally ill.

I was part of a ten-member team sent to the school attended by the student who shot himself at the quarry. We blanketed the whole school with an in-house workshop on suicide. The students received no advance warning about the visitors or the topic, for fear that some would stay away. The team's message was: "It could be your friend who will need your help."

Because most children turn to their peers when they feel suicidal, it is important to present relevant information to help students understand and cope with their friends' needs. Not surprisingly, most of the students found the day shocking, depressing, and uncomfortable.

However, another time I gave a workshop on suicide at a high school "lifestyles" day. Since mine was one of forty available options, I expected perhaps twenty participants. There were over two-hundred!

What we need to know

Why do children consider death? How are we to deal with the messages sent our way about their despair and their longing to end their life? What clues will help us to recognize that a child is drifting in the direction of self-destruction?

Writer and researcher Angela Gillis says: "Adolescent suicide is the last resort in a long line of unsuccessful efforts to achieve what is needed, by the child who is reaching out to be wanted, needed, and loved by others." *Wanted, needed, and loved.* Many grieving parents respond in confusion: "He *was* loved. Didn't he see it?" "We appreciated her so much. We told her all the time."

But it is the perception of the child that counts. Once my adolescent students created a collection of poetry about their feelings, which we sent home (no names shown) for their parents to read and comment on. Many of those poems saddened me. The students wrote about not being told they were loved and not being able to tell their parents, of not feeling wanted, appreciated, or understood.

At the beginning of my guidance unit on self-esteem, I ask the students to head their notebooks, in capital letters, with these words:

I, [NAME], AM A WONDERFUL, BEAUTIFUL, UNIQUE HUMAN BEING. I AM CAPABLE AND LOVABLE.

I know that many do not believe this about themselves. But I also know that behind much of the acting-out behavior we see — the clinging to each other, the bravado, and the posturing — lies this message: "Tell me I matter."

Of course, most children, even those with low self-esteem, do not kill themselves. Most children have enough resources, either within themselves or from their peer group and family, to survive. But some children do not survive, and others might not without the right help at the right time. Gillis adds: "Suicidal adolescents feel rejected and alone, unappreciated and unloved. Their fear of failure and rejection becomes so great that they choose to face death rather than continue facing life." So many teen suicides follow breakups with girlfriends or boyfriends, committed by fragile egos who are not able to face the pain.

What can we do?

The good news is that many potential tragedies can be prevented if parents, teachers, and students learn more about suicide. *Any talk of suicide must be heeded.* The teacher's first reaction to the middle-of-the-night wrist-cutting story was disbelief and scepticism. Common responses are: "She didn't really mean to do it. She was probably very careful not to cut too deeply. She's just vying for attention, trying to punish her family." The horror is that we will never know how many adolescents have died when all they really wanted to do was get attention or say, "I'll make you sorry." How many families have to face the rest of their lives knowing, afterward, that the clues and threats were there before, unheeded? Most successful suicides have been preceded by at least one unsuccessful attempt.

So, what do we need to be aware of? Here's a list of behavioral changes from a helpful book entitled *Preventing Adolescent Suicide* that might provide clues. Some, you may observe yourself; others, parents and peers might tell you about. You will notice how similar many of them are to those on previous lists, but they are worth repeating. We should watch for:

- a dramatic shift in academic performance
- changes in social behavior — turning into a loner, for instance
- changes in daily behavior and living patterns — turning messy, tardy, or rude, for instance
- extreme fatigue or unusual signs of boredom
- decreased appetite, loss of weight
- excessive daydreaming and inability to concentrate
- overt signs of mental illness — having hallucinations or talking to themselves, for instance
- giving away treasured possessions (usually considered a critical sign)
- truancy
- excessive use of drugs or alcohol

- growing failure to communicate with family and teachers
- morose, rebellious, or destructive behavior
- focusing on death in talking and writing

These behaviors might signify nothing worse than the normal pattern of temporary teenage unhappiness, but our antenna should always be out in case they are signs of more serious problems. They become of more concern if they are set next to any of the following family or personal situations:

- family problems: alcoholism, unavailable parents, violence in the home, unemployment of a parent, marital conflict, separation, or divorce
- peer difficulties: losing a best friend, being pressured to conform
- breakup of a romance
- stresses of growing up: unreasonable demands to excel (many top kids attempt suicide for this reason)
- identity concerns: sexuality, negative body image
- lack of a father-son relationship because of death, divorce, or career requirements
- difficult mother-daughter relationship, especially if a strong father figure is absent
- pregnancy, especially if the girl's boyfriend or parents have rejected her

Some children come to school considerably more at risk than others. Children in the following situations are at particular risk.

- Children from families whose religious beliefs or cultural practices make them appear different from other families in the community.

- Children from families that place great importance on social status and material gains.
- Children who are unwanted.
- Children who constantly carry adult burdens, particularly the oldest child who may feel responsible for the emotional tone of the family.
- Children of parents who use threats and rejection to gain compliance, who neglect their children, or who practice psychological or physical abuse.
- Only children who have no sense of self-worth.

Every year we know or hear about a few children whose situation or behavior puts them on the "potential" list. Others we may never recognize.

Talk about suicide or death is a key indicator, especially if the words indicate some sort of plan. The child who asks a friend to walk with her to the nearby railway tracks and play a certain song by a certain group just before a train is due is a high-risk child! By far the majority of children confide in their friends, and workshops like the one I mentioned earlier are critical to break the "friends don't tell" mentality. *Friends need to tell.*

What can you do if you or others in the school pick up danger signals? Let me first give you a list of things to *not* do.

- Don't condemn the child for having suicidal feelings.
- Don't assume the child is not the suicidal type.
- Don't be cheerful and say that things will get better.
- Don't allow the child to be left alone if you believe the risk is high. Many suicides take place at home between 3:30 PM and midnight.

- Don't ever give in to requests for secrecy.

   Now for the things you *should* do:

- If the subject presents itself, for example, in a current events session, use the opportunity to talk about suicide. Look for kits and resources that will help you. Stress the fact that suicidal feelings are often short-term and will pass. Constantly reinforce the invitation to approach you or another adult for help.

- If children confide feelings that might indicate suicidal intentions, listen carefully and offer some coping strategies. If I am especially worried about a child, I may come right out and ask, "Are you thinking of hurting yourself?" I follow my inner feelings as an observant, caring adult.

   Alert guidance departments are especially attentive to the pattern of a suicide, for they know how the suicide of one child can trigger others. Psychologist Dr. Robert Vinci has said about the role of schools in preventing suicides: "Adolescent suicide is a complex issue and affects not only the victims but the people around them. It is clear we need to improve our understanding of this issue. As teachers and educators, we are challenged to stem the tide of this phenomenon."

   He offers the following suggestions.

- Get involved. Push your administration to promote programs to educate both staff and students.
- Work to understand the complexities of adolescent development and the multiple issues they must deal with.
- Recognize the signs and symptoms of adolescent depression.

- Be available to your students and open to communication from them. (I would add a reminder of the power of journals as a means of communication.)
- Be aware of community resources and appropriate ways of referring a child and/or family to the correct agency.

Since Vinci's suggestions were published, many school boards, especially large ones, have put some sort of crisis intervention team in place, and many schools have formulated their own plan of action. Whether or not your school has established procedures, much of what I said earlier about school responses to death from accident or illness is applicable to suicide as well. Let me briefly summarize by way of describing what happened in one school.

The day after a boy's suicide, the students and teacher from his home room and from some other classes that knew him well suspended their planned curriculum. The teacher first provided time for his classmates to share their feelings, and then left individual students free to meet in small groups for the rest of the day. A few teachers were available to talk with any students who wanted to talk and to monitor how they were handling the situation. Those students known to be at risk were given special attention by members of the guidance department. In some cases, the parents were alerted. In the meantime, plans were made for the school's participation in the funeral. A dance scheduled for the following night was canceled. The whole school community breathed an air of sincere caring.

Again, I want to remind you how important your own feelings are. It is not easy to distinguish between the quite common mention of suicide by students when they are down and the deeper symptoms I have referred to. If your own feelings are unclear, or if you feel uncertain, call on your principal or board resource person for help. We must not gamble with the precious lives of our young people. We are not psychologists and must never take it upon ourselves to try to "fix" a child we feel is in true despair.

Our greatest contribution to prevention is the steady, constant, and deliberate building of self-esteem in our students. Our ongoing acceptance of them and our genuine caring for them are the most effective antidotes we can give children against the terrible loneliness they often feel. Perhaps we cannot change many of the circumstances in the world they inhabit outside school, but we can at least make school a friendlier place for them. Let us never be too busy to do that.

Suicide

Resources for Adults

AFTER SUICIDE, John Hewett, Westminster Press, 1980.

COPING WITH TEENAGER DEPRESSION, Kathleen McCoy, Dutton, 1985.

"Early Detection of the Suicidal Adolescent," Angela Gillis, Psychiatric Nursing, October/November, 1984.

PLEASE LISTEN TO ME: A GUIDE TO UNDERSTANDING TEENAGERS AND SUICIDE, Self-Counsel Press, 1992.

SUICIDAL CHILD, Cynthia R. Pfeffer, Guilford Press, 1986.

SUICIDE: GUIDANCE FOR GRADES 1-8, Anita Russell and Karen Rayter, Peguis Publishers, 1989.

WHY ISN'T JOHNNY CRYING? COPING WITH DEPRESSION IN CHILDREN, Donald McKnew, W. W. North & Co, 1985.

Resources for Children

COPING WITH SUICIDE, Judie Smith, Rosen Group, 1990. (grades 7-12)

DEGRASSI TALKS: DEPRESSION, Boardwalk Books, Mint Publishers & Toronto Sun, 1992. (ages 10-16)

KIDS HELP PHONE 1-800-668-6868 (Canada)

SUICIDE HOTLINE 1-800-333-5580 (U.S.)

WHEN LIVING HURTS, Sol Gordon, Dell, 1988. (grades 5,6 and up)

Separation and Divorce

She was in hysterics in the girls' washroom. Her dad had moved out a few days earlier, and this morning there'd been a strange man in her mother's bedroom.

• • • • •

She had been snatched from the school playground by her non-custodial mother. Later she lived with her grandparents, but they didn't want her to be part of the school support group because she had a good home and was not one of "those." She became more and more troubled and was eventually expelled from high school for missing a whole semester.

• • • • •

My principal heard sobbing coming from the boys' washroom and brought a weeping seven-year-old to me. I took him on my knee and he told me that his daddy had come home to try again and everything had been so great. Then his parents had another fight and his father moved out for good the night before.

• • • • •

I could fill a whole book with similar stories. For a number of years I have run noon-hour support groups for children affected by separation and divorce and listened to them tell me their heartbreaking stories.

Of all the issues in this book, this is the most personal for me. I have lived separation and divorce. Before I went through that anguish myself, I did not know how painful things like holidays can be. How can joy be complete when time together is limited at both ends? From Christmas Eve until Christmas day noon, the children are with one parent, and then, no matter what, they're sent off to the other. Before, I did not know about the singles subculture, the dances, the Single Parent Association, the pain *and* the recovery. Only one colleague knew what my life was really like during that terrible period — I could not face having the others know. I even transferred to another school the following year so I would not be around when they found out.

Most of the teachers who attend my night course on this topic tell me that they cover up the same way I did. They all hurt and need to be with others who understand the anguish they are experiencing.

The process of grieving takes two to five years if you work at it, longer if you do not. A key factor is owning up to the sorrow, the pain, the anger, the guilt, and the feelings of rejection you experience. This kind of grieving is terribly egocentric. The parents themselves need support, and they often find it difficult to provide the support their children need as they watch their security shatter.

In a sense, children lose both parents when one parent dies or leaves — the one who remains will never be the same again. I watched my youngest, then sixteen, wailing out her rage and grief when her father left: "How could he do this to me?" Many years later she still expresses the wish to be "back there" when her mom read and baked cookies and was always home when she was needed.

Children grieve just as hard as grown-ups do. As Suzy Yehl Marta, founder of the Rainbows for All God's Children program puts it, the hearts of children are the same size as ours, and they hurt just as much. She also reminds us that children learn from the heart up — if they are hurting, they simply cannot learn.

The problems children face

Despite the smiling newspaper photos, the wonderful weddings, the hopes and dreams, half of the marriages begun in the 80s and 90s will end in divorce. The wounded children are — and will be — with us, and they are often very fragile.

Imagine the effect on a newly separated child when the PA system announces: "Please make sure you take this letter home to your mom and dad." Imagine the class making cards for Father's or Mother's Day, when some children may not even know where their father or mother lives anymore. Imagine always having to give the teacher's "Dear Parents" notes to your grandmother because you never see your mother at all and your father only on weekends.

Some children in your class may live with a parent who doesn't date, some with a parent who does. Some may live with one parent and a boyfriend or girlfriend. In some cases, the parent's new partner may be the same sex as the parent. Others may live in a blended family with a stepmom or stepdad and new brothers and sisters. Some you may know about; some you may not. Until the last week of school one year, I didn't know that the parents of two boys in my grade eight class had remarried. Their files simply said "living with both parents."

Some children daily experience horrendous, draining home situations, often with the parents battling over custody and support payments. A woman once said to me, "How do I feel about my nearly ex-husband? Murder is the word. If I could kill him and get away with it, I would. I hate him." Ask yourself how her son is doing in school.

Recently I chided a boy for not doing anything during a whole writing period. Normally a bright and eager student, he seemed suddenly unmotivated and vague. Later he told me that he had returned from a visit to his dad the day before, "and all the bad things he said about Mom kept going around and around in my head." Children hate it when one parent denigrates the other. They also hate having to carry messages: "Tell your dad to get that support payment in or else." They hate being made to spy: "What woman is he seeing now? What is she like?"

As explained in the Rainbows for All God's Children training session, not only do children of divorce suffer severe stress, they also incur serious losses. For instance:

• Their view of reality has been shattered. A home with two parents is secure, even if the parents fight. Now the children must rebuild, often during a time when both parents are emotionally unavailable to them. Most children remember exactly where they were and what they were doing when they were told. Some, of course, were never told anything until one day one parent was gone.

- Often divorce forces a move or a reduced standard of living. Losses may include home, school, friends, and neighborhood. I now recall the period before my divorce as a time of middle-class smugness: house, two incomes, and no financial worries. After their dad left, my kids referred to me as "a single parent trying to keep her family together almost on welfare." We could afford to joke, for even though we had to cut back some, I was well paid. Many families in similar circumstances have to learn to live on half of what they have been used to, or less. Single mothers are among the poorest people in North America.

- Sometimes siblings are split up between the parents. The additional loss of one or more siblings makes life even more lonely and painful.

- Often a whole extended family is lost. I talk to children who never see the grandparents, aunts, and uncles on one side.

- Familiar routines are lost. Holidays are never the same. Birthdays, anniversaries, graduation may now all be tense times. Will they see or hear from the absent parent?

- Custody arrangements can cause heartbreaking loss of a close parent-child relationship. When parents aren't allowed to see their children often enough, the time they do spend together tends to become superficial, filled with treats and events instead of real relating. Some parents disappear from their children's lives for extended periods, some forever. The

men in my night class taught me a male viewpoint —
their emotions are torn each time they have to return
the children. (Roughly 85 percent of children live
with their mothers.)

- Children wish intensely for reconciliation. "I was
that close," a young boy told his support group, crying as he put his thumb and index finger together.
The others in the group nodded. Many parents try
living together again, but if the attempt is unsuccessful, the final separation may cause even deeper
heartaches. Some children feel ashamed because
they do not have a "real family" anymore.

- Sadly, it is rare for separated or divorced parents to
have an amicable relationship. Too often they do not
even tolerate each other anymore. I always tell children that their parents loved each other once — it
just did not work out.

- Most children have difficulty adjusting to the new
love interest in one or both parents' lives — they
often refer to "my real dad" or "my real mom" — and
intensely dislike their stepsiblings. They find it
painful to see their parent play mom or dad to
strangers. Divorce rates for second marriages are
higher than for first marriages. The complexities of
parenting other people's sometimes embittered children and the financial stresses of separated and
divorced families are often too much for the second
marriage to bear.

The results

TVOntario, an educational public service chan-
nel, has produced a program called *Divorce: A Family*

Crisis. The teacher's guide says: "Although research shows that the first two years after the separation are the most stressful because the parent-child relationship is under the greatest strain, the longer term effects are disturbing. After eight years, over a third are still depressed." The following information supports that statement:

- Children's initial response to divorce depends on their age and development at the time of the breakup. By understanding age-specific reactions and knowing what to expect, parents are better able to help each child.

- Older kids experience fears about their future relationships. Many children of divorce do go on to unsuccessful marriages of their own, especially if emotional issues remain unresolved.

- As a result of marital conflict and divorce, many children do not perceive themselves as wanted, needed, or loved. These perceptions are contributing factors in many teenage suicides.

- Many psychologists maintain that divorce is harder for children to deal with than the death of a parent. People involved in divorce do not experience the same compassion and support that those who suffer the death of a parent or spouse receive. Perhaps this accounts for the secrecy that often surrounds separation and divorce.

Nevertheless, most children do learn to cope. A boy in one of my classes always insisted that his parents were not separated, that his dad was away only because of his work, until one day he was able to admit that he lived with just his mom. His openness prompted another girl to share a problem she had about her dad's girlfriend. Another talked about how fellow students teased her with "You don't have a father anymore." These children were comforted by the knowledge that they were not alone in their unhappy circumstances.

In fact, many students are lucky enough to come through all the turmoil and flourish relatively unscathed. I know some wonderful one-parent homes and blended families, filled with mature people who are dedicated to their children's needs as well as their own. I know of biological parents who carefully work out what is best for the children, get along, are faithful about schedules, provide a true "home" on both sides. With kind and caring support, some children of divorce remain or quickly become very stable.

What can we do?

When the time came that I was able to see past my own pain-blurred circumstances, I became concerned about others in similar pain. I discovered that nothing was being done in my school.

I took out the big binder in the office that contains permission forms and made a list of all the children who came from a background of death, separation, or divorce. With the support of the principal, I set out to establish noon-hour support meetings for children in grades four to eight. (I was not sure how to handle primary children.) The principal insisted on permission forms for the younger students, but only one mother refused to allow her child to attend. We met every two weeks to share stories, happenings, books, and a filmstrip series, but it was just being together that mattered the most. I soon began a primary group as well, and their enthusiasm was amazing. Every day a few little ones would stop me in the hall to ask if it was get-together day. They particularly liked the name we came up with: the Sunshine Club.

The older group eventually joined Rainbows for All God's Children, an after-school support group that meets for twelve weeks, including two Saturday sessions. Trained facilitators work with a maximum of six children, using workbooks, games, and other material to cover a large number of topics. I was trained by the founder, Suzy Yehl Marta, and oversee the program in several nearby schools. What I like most about the program is the one-hour workshop on how children grieve. It is for all school staff, including secretaries, bus drivers, yard supervisors, custodians — anyone who deals with the children. The school bears the cost, although parents are invited to make donations if they can. The program has two versions, one religious and one secular, both with well-planned themes and lessons.

Helping those who don't want help

These and other support-group meetings help many children, but not all choose to participate. Some children do not like being singled out, especially as they get to be teenagers. Some parents do not want their children to share "personal family business." We have to respect these wishes, but that does not mean that we cannot look for other ways to help. Being a careful and caring listener, suggesting appropriate books, and talking about feelings during class discussions are basic strategies that will help children cope.

I also try to keep these more specific strategies in mind as I deal with hurting children.

- Reinforce again and again that separation and divorce are grown-up decisions, not caused by the child.

- Help the children to understand that anger is part of the process of grieving, a necessary part. Help them to separate their anger at the *behavior* of a parent from the love they have for the *person*. So many people do not understand the difference.

- Allow the children to express their feelings freely, as long as their words and deeds do not harm themselves, or others, or the tone of the classroom.

- Arrange for a place where the children can go when they feel overcome with sadness or anger. In my school, the library is that place. They can talk to the librarian or just sit and look at magazines. I often give time-out certificates to children in crisis.

- It sometimes helps to twin an older child of divorce with a newly separated one and invite them to go off in a corner and exchange stories. The newer one will see that there is "life after . . ."

- Show sympathy, but not pity. Say: "It's hard right now. You must feel confused (or sad or angry, depending on their behavior). That's okay. These feelings won't last forever, but it's important to feel them now."

- Be especially alert for outbursts of anger and suggest appropriate strategies to help the children cope with their strong feelings.

- Inform all school staff of children who are experiencing difficulties. We put sticky notes up behind the copier, alerting everyone to a fragile child who needs kindness.

- Be vigilant for a long time. A child on the road to recovery is likely to be swept up in emotion again when the final divorce is granted, or when a birthday or other significant event passes without a word from the absent parent.

- Communicate to the children that they cannot use their situation to get out of responsibilities. Provide whatever academic assistance is necessary but do not do their work for them. Expect a lowering of standards for a while, then gently urge a renewed focus on work as a good outlet. Some children manage to put home circumstances out of their mind while they are at school and continue to do very well, but this takes great emotional energy.

- Sometimes one or both parents will come in to see you, wanting reassurance that their child is receiving caring support. They may just need to talk — an opportunity to use your active listening skills. Whether or not a parent comes in, a note home saying that you are looking after the child in a special way will be much appreciated.

I was on duty one day, walking with a grade four girl on each hand. One was telling me about her parents' divorce. The other listened, then said, "My parents aren't divorced yet." The first girl's response was "They will be." Children learn to be survivors at a very early age. They learn to adapt and sometimes to be more careful in their own later relationships. I see this in my own children. They are cautious about serious relating and I think that is a good thing.

One unexpected benefit of divorce is that parents often become more real to their children, more accessible. Instead of mom-and-dad, each parent becomes an individual, and the opportunities for a close friendship between parent and child increase immeasurably. It is the interim that is so difficult, the bridge between the before life and the new life. That is where we are needed.

Separation and Divorce

Resources for Adults

HELPING YOUR CHILD SUCCEED AFTER DIVORCE, Florence Bienenfeld, Hunter House, 1987.

LOVE IN THE BLENDED FAMILY: FALLING IN LOVE WITH A PACKAGE DEAL, Angela N. Clubb, N.C. Press and Health Communications, 1990.

SECOND CHANCES: MEN, WOMEN AND CHILDREN A DECADE AFTER DIVORCE WHO WINS, WHO LOSES - AND WHY, Sandra Blakeslee and Judith S. Wallerstein, Ticknor & Fields, 1990.

Resources for Children

DINOSAUR'S DIVORCE: A GUIDE FOR CHANGING FAMILIES, Laurene and Mark Brown, Little, Brown, 1988. (preschool - grade 3)

DO I STILL HAVE A DADDY? Jeanne Warren Lindsay, Morning Glory Press, 1990. (grades 1-2)

EVERYTHING YOU NEED TO KNOW ABOUT STEPFAMILIES, Bruce Glassman, Rosen Group, 1991. (grades 7-12)

HOW IT FEELS WHEN PARENTS DIVORCE, Jill Krementz, Knopf, 1984. (grades 4-9)

LIVING WITH A SINGLE PARENT, Richard Mancini, Rosen Group, 1991. (grades 7-12)

ME AND MY STEPFAMILY: A KID'S JOURNAL, Ann Banks, Puffin, 1990.

WHAT'S GOING TO HAPPEN TO ME? - WHEN PARENTS SEPARATE OR DIVORCE, Eda LeShan, Macmillan Child Group, 1986. (grades 3-7)

WHEN YOUR PARENTS GET A DIVORCE: A KID'S JOURNAL, Ann Banks, Puffin, 1990.

PART III

ALCOHOLISM

"Just the way she gets out of the car, I know," said one student. "It's like she's two people."

• • • • •

"She makes me lie for her," said another. "I have to answer the door when the landlord comes for the rent and say she's not home. I hate it. I hate it worse when she's drunk."

• • • • •

In a drunken rage the father had put his arm through the window. It took sixteen stitches to close the wound. The teacher sent the student to the library for a time-out, since there was no way she could concentrate on her work.

• • • • •

"Sometimes I yell at him to go away and leave us alone," one boy admitted. He refuses to do his schoolwork. His father batters him when he's drinking.

• • • • •

An estimated 1.5 million to 2 million Canadians are alcoholics. The life of each alcoholic has an impact on the lives of seven to fourteen other people: family members, co-workers, relatives, friends, and neighbors.

John Bradshaw, psychologist, writer, and non-drinking alcoholic (alcoholics do not talk about being cured), says that alcohol is the leading killer in North America. It causes heart attacks and liver diseases, as well as what he calls "car murders," and is linked to much physical violence — approximately two-thirds of the children of alcoholics are beaten. One-half of the fathers who commit incest are alcoholics. Alcohol is a powerfully addictive drug that affects the part of the brain that controls emotional responses. Bradshaw defines addiction as "any pathological relationship with any mood-altering experience that has life-damaging consequences," and gives his own experience as an example. He used to drink to solve the problems caused by his drinking.

This chapter may reach some of you on a very personal level. Perhaps you live with an alcoholic or teach with one. Alcoholics are everywhere — in schools, universities, hospitals, businesses. Some, like bus drivers, train engineers, and pilots, have responsibilities that affect the safety of others. The numbers are frightening:

- one in three children of an alcoholic becomes one
- one in five high school students drinks daily
- one in three teenagers is classified as a problem drinker
- only one in thirty-seven alcoholics admits to being one and goes for treatment

How many alcoholics are in your neighborhood? Count one house out of every six. How many students in a class are likely to have an alcoholic parent? There are four or five in any medium-sized class. But you probably will not find it easy to recognize which four or five they are. These children are often called "the invisible victims," since the first family rule is: "Don't tell."

Unfortunately, our culture often represents drunkenness as funny. Famous comedians such as Carol Burnett and Dudley Moore have made weaving and slurred speech seem hilarious. It should come as no surprise, then, that children often laugh uproariously at any suggestion of lack of control, whether from this or some other condition. It is easy to ignore the pain behind the slurred speech. But children from alcoholic homes know the pain of seeing their parent become that "other" person who is abusive, mean, and dangerous.

We need to accept that those four or five students are there, whether we recognize them or not. And we need to learn what life is like for them, so we can give them the help and understanding they need.

Alcoholic homes

An alcoholic family is a dysfunctional family, as are many of the families I alluded to earlier in the chapters on physical and sexual abuse. John Bradshaw describes dysfunctional families as "frozen mobiles." Healthy family mobiles sway and reassemble; dysfunctional family mobiles do not.

Dysfunctional families deny the five family freedoms (first suggested by Virginia Satir, pioneer family systems psychologist: the power to perceive, to think and interpret, to feel, to want and choose, to imagine. Here are some of the "rules" that Bradshaw claims govern the life of a dysfunctional family.

- Control all interactions, feelings, and personal behavior at all times.
- Always be right in everything you do, or at least believe you are right.
- Blame others first, and when things don't go right, blame yourself.
- Don't talk, especially not about feelings, needs, or wants.
- Reframe hurt, pain, and distress in ways that will distract others from knowing what is really happening.
- Don't make mistakes; they reveal your flawed, vulnerable self.
- Don't expect reliability. Don't trust anyone and you'll never be disappointed.
- Keep the same disagreements going on for years.

Bradshaw believes that all families are dysfunctional to some degree, since there are no "perfect" parents. Every family is somewhere on a continuum from very supportive and free to totally imprisoned. Any addiction plays a role in family dysfunction. Parents who are addicted to work, to eating, or to gambling are parents who are unavailable to their children. Their addiction is their number-one priority, not the physical and psychological health of their family.

Alcoholic dysfunction

A drug counselor friend (an alcoholic himself) says he can easily spot alcoholics in a bar. They get very nervous when their glasses get down to a third full, and look around frantically for a refill. Interestingly, my friend did the same with his coffee while we were at dinner! This man took me to two AA meetings and I attended six AlAnon gatherings, where I heard heart-rending tales about the depths to which people must sink before they voice the first of the twelve AA steps: "I have a problem." Dysfunctional alcoholic families sustain the myth that the parent or parents can stop at any time and can handle their drinking. But the truth is that booze runs the home.

Key to understanding alcoholism is the fact that *the drinking is harming the drinker or others around him or her, but the drinker will not stop.* Not all alcoholics drink all the time or have binges every weekend. Some have no more than two drinks a day, and some drink heavily only once a month. But they are still alcoholics. Imagine a horizontal line across a chalkboard or a piece of paper. On the far left is the non-drinker, on the right the skid row bum — only 5 percent of all alcoholics. Somewhere in between, an alcoholic person will cross the critical point from *wanting* a drink to *needing* one.

Are alcoholics born or made? Probably both. One type of alcoholic inherits a genetic weakness or predis-position — some teens become alcoholics when they take their first drink. A second type becomes addicted after a long period of use. Children of alcoholics have a much greater chance of becoming alcoholics them-selves, and the probability is high that they will marry one as well, even if they themselves do not drink.

What makes an alcoholic? Who is an alcoholic? What do alcoholics feel and think? I offer the following profile of alcoholics.

- They don't like themselves or their world, so they drink to change both.
- They deny that their actions have consequences. A bad situation is always someone else's foul-up.

- They think of their own needs, "me only."
- They refuse to accept factual information.
- They have very little moral fiber. They will lie and steal when they have to.
- They have little respect for those closest to them or in positions of power in their lives — including spouses and parents.
- They overreact regularly due to a low tolerance of frustation and a need for immediate gratification.

Not all of these factors may be obvious all the time, of course. But alcoholism is progressive in its severity, and over time all will be seen and felt by the families.

Children from alcoholic homes

Some of our students have memories of the time before alcohol began to rule their family, while others have always lived in tension. Imagine never being able to bring a friend home. Imagine always having to protect the family through secrecy, lies, and manipulation. Imagine what it's like to have parents whose behavior is unpredictable, often violent. Imagine living with a parent who gives you little or no love, security, or guidance; who loads you down with blame and makes promises that aren't kept. Imagine the tearing of a child's heart when the safe, loving, good parent takes the bottle from the shelf and, once again, Mr. or Ms. Hyde emerges.

Recognizing these children

It isn't easy to spot children from alcoholic homes. Different children compensate for their problems in different ways, but the following set of profiles is one that many specialists, including Claudia Black and Sharon Wegsheider Cruise, agree on. It may alert you to possible problems behind the observable behavior of your students.

Perfectionists

Perfectionists believe that parental alcoholism will not be blamed on them if they stand out: become superior academically, a leader in sports, class president, extra attractive. Oldest children tend to become perfectionists. "Family hero" figures badly need attention from the outside world to cover up a deep sense of failure inside. Teachers often love these superkids, but the other students may find them overly serious and boring.

Peacemakers

Peacemakers are the diplomats of the family. They soothe the hurts, cover up, learn to put themselves last, work for compromise, and try to understand the alcoholic parent. This is the child who cleans up the messes, listens to the complaints of other family members, tries above all to avoid conflict, and learns to keep hurts and angers inside. Teachers value peacemakers, and peers find them loyal and helpful. As adults, they are often used by others.

Withdrawers

Withdrawers hide, becoming hermits at home and loners at school. They are the quiet and unobtrusive students we do not get to know. They may withdraw into a private world of television, computers, books, or music. Academically they are average students who aim to avoid attention and conflict. Drugs and alcohol can become their secret friends.

Distractors (clowns)

Distractors are the jokers, the hyperactive ones, the constant talkers, the troublemakers, or the whiners. They divert the family's attention from the alcoholic problems to themselves. Usually the youngest, these children mask the terror they feel with nervous energy. They become manipulative, charming, selfish — very afraid, insecure people.

Rebels

Rebels are the toughies and sometimes the family scapegoats. They are the ones into drugs, sex, and drinking. Admired by a certain group of peers who become a surrogate family, they are the school's under-achievers and office-bench-sitters. They appear to have concluded that negative strokes are better than no strokes at all. We watch these kids head out from our classrooms toward hardship, drug dependency, early pregnancy, welfare, jail, or suicide.

Any of these children may need our help to cope with the burdens of a dysfunctional family. Our first task is to spot them. It is especially easy to overlook the perfectionist and the peacemaker, for instance, since they do not appear to be troubled children. Once you recognize the anxiety (and anger!) in these children, it may be harder to know how to help without adding to their already difficult situation.

What can we do?

If so many of these children do not want to be noticed, do not want to be helped, then what is our responsibility? What can we do to lessen their emotional pain?

First and foremost, we need to find them. Then we need to gain their trust. Here are some strategies to consider.

- Listen without judging, becoming the outlet they need. With many, that may be all we can do. But that is already a lot — their sense of aloneness is debilitating.

- Help them to believe that they are not to blame, even if they have been told that they're the cause of the problem. Alcoholism in the family is an adult problem, and nothing they did or do now makes one whit of difference.

- Assure them that nagging the drinker will not work, nor will arguing, pleading, bargaining, hiding the booze, or dumping it down the sink.

- Discuss with them how covering up enables the person to continue drinking.

- Point out that the problem belongs to the drinker and only the drinker can solve it.

- Help them to develop a life outside of the family. These children desperately need friendship, need to be invited into other homes where family life is calm. We cannot manipulate children into friendship, but sometimes we can arrange to pair hurting children with stable, open, friendly partners.

- Help them to look after their own needs by showing them how frustration and anger can be released in healthy ways.

- Encourage them to share their feelings, by talking and writing in journals, for instance.

- Make them aware of relevant books and other materials, and let them know about Alateen, the support group for children.

- Give the whole class information on alcoholism in general and coping techniques in particular, hoping it may help those who are too afraid to disclose. Some children simply do not know that life in their family is not normal family life.
- Above all, be watchful and available. Call outside agencies when you suspect abuse or neglect.

Fortunately, more and more good teaching material is becoming available from commercial publishers and from school authorities. There are associations like Lions-Quest Canada that fund programs to help adolescents acquire skills for making decisions, solving problems, and dealing with feelings. There are people out there like you who care enough to be supportive and concerned. Children from alcoholic families have a special need for your love and respect, and to learn the value of human worth.

Alcoholism

Resources for Adults

HEALING THE SHAME THAT BINDS YOU, John Bradshaw, Health Communications, 1988.

CHILDREN ARE PEOPLE TOO - A Comprehensive Elementary School Substance Abuse Prevention Curriculum and Support Group Training Program for Children Between Ages 5-12. Canada (416)360-5296, U.S. 1-800-851-9100.

LIONS QUEST - Self-esteem building and substance abuse prevention program for children. Canada 1-800-265-2680, U.S. 1-800-288-6401.

NATIONAL ALCOHOL HOT-LINE — 1-800-ALCOHOL (U.S.)

Resources for Children

DEGRASSI TALKS: ALCOHOL, Boardwalk Books Inc, Mint Publishers & Toronto Sun, 1992. (ages 9-16)

EVERYTHING YOU NEED TO KNOW ABOUT AN ALCOHOLIC PARENT, Nancy Shuker, Rosen Group, 1989. (grades 7-12)

NO WAY SLIPPERY SLICK - A CHILD'S FIRST BOOK ABOUT DRUGS, Bank Street College, Harper Collins, 1991. (ages 4-8)

TARGET — HELPING STUDENTS COPE WITH ALCOHOL AND OTHER DRUGS. 1-800-366-6667 (U.S.)

WHEN YOUR PARENT DRINKS TOO MUCH: A BOOK FOR TEENAGERS, Eric Ryerson, Warner, 1987.

POVERTY

*Conversation with this shy thirteen-year-old was like digging
a garden with a spoon. But one day his words and tears
flowed. Mom hadn't received the welfare check because of a
bureaucratic mixup and Dad, separated and far away,
wouldn't help. There was no money in the house and almost
no food. I called the mother, recommended the food bank, and
gave her a phone number for immediate assistance.*

• • • • •

*A journal entry I was meant to read said that the electricity
was being cut off because there was no money to pay the bill.
Did they have food? Yes, but her dad was going to have to
get another job — he couldn't pay the bills for five of them on
minimum wage. The phone and cable were already gone.
Later the mother began to work nights and left the four-year-
old unsupervised while she slept during the day.*

• • • • •

*She missed her graduation because they had to move. The
mortgage payments were way behind.*

• • • • •

*One day he was in school and the next day the whole family
had disappeared. A credit collector friend told me it happens
all the time.*

• • • • •

I remember that we always had to be careful with money when I was a child. We did not own a car until I was seventeen. For my eighth Christmas I asked for skates. My mother explained that I needed a new snowsuit, but with the sublime faith of childhood I chose to believe that the large wrapped box under the tree contained my skates — white figure skates, of course. When I unpacked a maroon snowsuit on Christmas morning, I burst into tears.

That was my childhood. I can understand a lot of the frustration children of poverty must feel. However, teachers and other professionals dealing with children may have salaries ranging from good to excellent and benefits that mean security, now and in the future. We are removed and protected, if not isolated, from the world of poverty.

The extent of the problem

It is appalling that the statistics I used when I first worked on this material have already been superseded by even worse news. Unemployment rates are rising in both Canada and the United States. Traditional manufacturing jobs that have sustained the economic lives of many small and medium-sized communities are disappearing forever. Dwindling fish stocks and vanishing forests are limiting jobs for fishermen and loggers. In many areas of North America, one out of every four people may never find a job!

Even the media reports of decreased unemployment receive mixed reactions at best, since high-paying jobs are being replaced with others that pay marginally above minimum wage. Contrary to what many people believe, most poor families are headed by adults who work or who are actively searching for a job. Half of the single-parent families headed by women are poor, with an average income a little over half that of single-parent families headed by men. Women working full-time earn about two-thirds as much as men do. Almost half of single women are poor — a higher number if they are also elderly. The number of children living in low-income families is steadily rising. For every five children under sixteen, at least one lives in poverty. Few poor children finish high school, let alone attend university. And the cycle continues: the lower the level of education, the greater the chances of remaining or falling below the poverty line.

Poverty is everywhere, not just in crowded cities. In an article in the *Toronto Star*, a United Church minister described the world of the rural poor as filled with "tin-roofed tar-paper-and-shingle shacks, no running water, dirt floors, no insulation, wood-stove heating." He added: "Welcome to the Third World."

What we need to know

Children of poverty come to school without new sneakers and a fancy lunch box. They may not have had breakfast. Some may have no lunch or only margarine sandwiches. They have no money for the book fair, for trips and outings, for dances, or even for bristol board or paper for projects. They will not be transported to nearby libraries for research materials, and they will not likely find any books or magazines at home. Even if teachers quietly pay for class trips, even if schools provide breakfasts or hot lunches, the fact remains that our education system betrays these children from poor homes.

The first thing we need to face is the possibility that we may be biased against families and children caught in poverty. Letters to newspaper editors often attach words and phrases like "lazy," "immoral," "lawless," "lack of motivation," "welfare bums" to the poor. What are your own concepts of the life and world of the impoverished children in your contact?

The word that comes to my mind when I think of poverty is "terror." Terror. Poor people do not have enough food or clothing, or decent shelter. They do not have proper furnishings or equipment, recreation, education, clothing, medical care, reading material, personal care, or household funds. Imagine a newly separated woman whose lifestyle suddenly and dramatically shifts to include intense worry about all these things. It is difficult to comprehend the terror of that woman when she has only two dollars left and another long week before the next government check arrives.

Infant mortality and accidental death rates are twice as high among the poor; death from infectious disease, two-and-a-half times. Prenatal and postnatal malnutrition may permanently retard both physical and intellectual growth. Early learning comes with curiosity, with children playing and exploring while adults assist and challenge, but many parents — single working or both working — simply do not have enough time and energy to give to that kind of stimulation. Poor children arrive at school lacking the kind of broad life experiences the school values most and the kind of linguistic skills the school's learning materials require. School texts and readers are filled with middle-class situations; for poorer children the images and the language can be confusing. Inadequate nutrition may adversely affect the acquisition of reading and math skills.

It is dangerous to have middle-class expectations of all our students. Consider the children who come to us from a crowded apartment or trailer or house. Consider the family without a father, with siblings vying for a tired mother's time and attention. Consider the words used to discipline those children, the actions that tell them they aren't valued, and the feelings of worthlessness that result. Then consider the level of their fatigue and their awareness that they are not keeping up with the class.

Consider the effect on these children of urging them to work hard now so that ten or twelve years from now they will have a good job and live a good life. To a hungry kid, what meaning do such expectations have? Our values are more likely to invite frustration in these students than encouragement, or helplessness, anxiety, anger, rebellion. Our expectations often reinforce an already low level of self-esteem and a negative motivation for school learning. The children may become impulsive and physically aggressive, with little respect for the property of others and little sense of guilt for what they do to others.

It is clear that we need to revise the expectations schools have of children from poor homes, but in doing so we need to remain clear about this point: *Poor children do not come to school less capable of learning or doomed to fail.* Their problem is frequently no more serious than overcoming the great divide between home and school. For middle-class children, life at home flows quite naturally into life at school. For children of poverty, however, many aspects of school that other students take for granted need to be made explicit.

Many school boards and municipal authorities have initiated special programs for children of poor families. Unfortunately, the resources are seldom sufficient. Walter Sinclair, an elementary school principal, says: "I know what will help the children but the problem is there is never enough time, never enough resources to do these things. If teachers have time to work with children's problems on an individual basis, then we can do something very positive. But politicians and trustees say we can't afford to reduce class size. Maybe that's true, but what happens later? In the long run, it's cost efficient to spend the money now."

The Toronto Department of Health runs a successful program called Parents Helping Parents, where women who are trained in child development go out into the community to advise mothers on stimulating their preschoolers. But, psychologist Bea Asham says: "Every year, somewhere between two and eight thousand babies are born in Toronto who could use a program like this. We can't hope to help even a fraction of them with the resources we have."

What can we do?

First, we all need to do a bit of personal soul-searching about our own attitudes. How much of our classroom talk betrays our prejudices about the worthiness of jobs and lifestyles not our own? I want to share with you a recent example of my own carelessness, one that caused me great shame.

I was teaching a poetry lesson to another teacher's junior class. One thing I wanted to do was show the children how, by adding some interesting language, we could change a mundane sentence like "The man walked" into something vibrant and alive. Together we wove a narrative about a sad, lonely man trudging along a major highway, bereft because his love had left him for a . . . . One child suggested "garbage man" as a label that would show our derision. The poem was composed, we read it aloud with great gusto, and I left the room certain that the regular teacher admired my expertise as a teacher of poetry.

However, when we met in the staff room she told me that the father of one of the students used to be a garbage collector. In fact, he had regularly picked up my own! The teacher had watched the little girl's reaction but had decided not to say anything since she did not appear to be concerned. I still feel the pain of that day as I write this, however, and a deep regret for my insensitivity. And I am certain there have been other times as well when I have said or done something thoughtless and hurtful. I am trying very hard now not to make the same mistake again.

We have to begin to see *all* of our children as learners with equal claims on our professionalism. Author James Baldwin, a child of poverty himself, speaks to us all when he says: "If you, the teacher, feel that the child is valuable, that he has a right to be here, he will, very slowly sometimes, and by putting you through many a gruelling test, respond to that. And if you feel he is worthless, or if you pity him or condescend to him, he will fear that and he will feel that no matter what you say, what you do, or how you smile. He will never trust you; you will never be able to reach him, and he will never be able to learn anything from you."

It does not seem to matter what style of teaching we use, as long as it is genuine and consistent. It only seems to matter, as Baldwin indicates, that the child feels important to the teacher. Children of poverty can accept cranky teachers, but they are devastated by indifference.

I want to finish this chapter with a quote that I believe should be on the bulletin board of every staff room in the land, again from Baldwin: "Children are probably the toughest and most fragile beings in the world and, bar none, the most important. They are also the most exasperating, cunning, devious, self-centered, ruthless, unpredictable, and exhausting people in the world. A hard day's work in the mines can be less grueling than walking a child through the park. The reason, for me anyway, that a child is so difficult and so valuable — sacred really — is that while it is virtually impossible to fool a child, it is very easy to betray him."

Poverty

THE CHASM: THE LIFE AND DEATH OF A GREAT EXPERIMENT IN GHETTO EDUCATION, Robert Campbell, Greenwood, 1986.

"Easing the Plight of Poor Children," Leslie Frumm, Toronto Star, September 19, 1987.

"Poverty Hidden Away in Shack Along the Backroads of Toronto," Toronto Star, May 1, 1988.

SAVAGE INEQUALITIES: CHILDREN IN AMERICA'S SCHOOLS, Jonathan Kozol, Harper Collins, 1992.

RACISM

When she was six, this daughter of black parents wrote on the About the Author page of her book: "I have a beautiful face." Will she be able to hold onto that strong sense of self her parents have given her?

• • • • •

He is Ojibway, the adopted son of white parents. There are several other native kids living in his village. He tells me that periodically the town kids gang up on them and call them "niggers."

• • • • •

He came to our grade six class straight from Jamaica. He was very black and his speech was quite different. He caused a great stir on the playground because he was so unusual.

• • • • •

I am an Alberta-born WASP, a teacher in an area where the school population consists almost totally of children of British, French, Dutch, and other European backgrounds, so my personal experience with racism is limited. Still, I always made it a point of telling my own children that we needed to enrich our family with new friends from other cultures and other races.

Where are you in your acceptance of children whose skin color differs from yours? How high is your tolerance of their values, their outlook on life, their religious beliefs? Where are your students in their thinking about each other? I know that deep down we carry a lot of cultural baggage, and yet racism is also a very private and personal attitude.

I do not know the attitudes and practices of most of my fellow staff members, or of my school and board administrators, and they may not know mine. I suspect that the contents of our school library and some of our textbooks may not be free from racial bias. Recent media reports indicate that racism is widespread in our culture and a large, malevolent stain on our way of life.

A paper on Canadian human rights, put out by the University of Ottawa and the Canadian Labour Congress, describes racist currents in contemporary life this way:

Overt discrimination

This is the unashamed kind, as in organized hate groups such as neo-Nazis and the Ku Klux Klan.

"Nice guy" (or girl) discrimination

This is a more typically Canadian practice in which nice, conservative, people do things quietly and without fuss. Often, people who do not consider themselves bigots, but who want to hold onto the established social order, discriminate subtly. Landlords refuse to rent to ethnic people because other tenants might be upset. Employers reject non-white applicants because of possible negative reactions from existing employees. Businesses exclude patrons from certain racial groups because of the anticipation of lost revenue.

Systemic or institutional discrimination

This is the most pervasive and difficult to combat. It is impersonal, indirect, and often unintentional. Even when everyone is treated equally, systemic discrimination can take place in a school board or industry that has had values embedded over time. The system treats society as if it were homogeneous, without recognizing or giving value to ethnic differences.

I believe that I neither show nor think open prejudice. I hope I am not guilty of practicing discrimination, even the "nice girl" kind. But I fear I am part of a systemic bias. I know I have let far too many opportunities go by to focus on or celebrate the differences particular students have represented. If equal treatment is unfair, then I have been unfair. I have taught a number of native students over the years, and I do not recall ever truly inviting them to share their heritage — or to investigate it in those instances when the children were seemingly "mainstream." Now that I am more aware, I can no longer excuse this behavior in myself.

Racism in education

The education system I work in reflects predominantly white, middle-class, mostly northern European values. Its curriculum contains little that relates to minority children or reflects their heroes, cultural diversity, and strengths. As I reflect on my own years of using readers with junior and intermediate classes, I ask myself where and how native, oriental, or French cultures were represented in my teaching.

Getting people to admit to their racist views is not easy. The Victoria County [Ontario] Board of

Education, a strong force in the field of racial equality, publishes a handbook that includes an escalating list of the prejudicial behaviors of teachers. With the permission of the superintendent, I present it as a possible personal gauge.

- non-intervention (witnessing an incident of harassment and not attempting to prevent it; not reporting it)
- exclusion (on racial grounds, avoiding or excluding any individual or any group from an activity)
- name-calling
- teasing and jokes that demean
- racial slurs or insults
- graffiti (degrading or insulting words, messages, slogans written in public places)
- derogatory material (writing, printing, or distributing it)
- vandalism of ethnic-owned material or property
- threats or terrorism
- physical violence

The history of North America contains many instances of racism, and in our teaching we must take ownership of key events, some well known, others not so prominent.

• • • • •

When railroads were being built across North America, Chinese men were brought in as cheap, abundant labor to lay the tracks through prairies and mountains. No wives were allowed to accompany their husbands because officials didn't want "those people" to settle here.

• • • • •

Both Japanese-Canadians and Japanese-Americans were put into concentration camps during World War II because they were considered a "security risk."

• • • • •

Canada accepted and welcomed British women and children evacuated during the bombing of London, but refused to let 907 Jewish refugees on the ship, St. Louis, land in 1939 after they had tried Cuba, Argentina, Uruguay, Paraguay, Panama, and the United States. The St. Louis was forced to sail back to Germany, where almost all of its passengers died in the gas chambers.

• • • • •

In British Columbia, homes of Indo-Canadian descent have been fire-bombed, their temples desecrated, their car windows smashed, and their children taunted and kicked.

• • • • •

These events and a great many more have been well documented in various sources. The following school incidents bring the problem even closer to our consciousness.

• • • • •

A grade four Sikh boy is called "turban head" and "towel head" and grabbed by two grade six boys who push snow into his face.

• • • • •

A seventeen-year-old black female student is called "jungle bunny," "African Zulu woman" and "nigger." One teacher nicknames her "Whoopi Snotberg."

• • • • •

In a letter to the school board, two parents report that their son has been repeatedly beaten, bashed against brick walls, and called all kinds of racially abusive names.

• • • • •

Systemic racism

Even more disheartening than the direct, personal racism in our schools are these examples of systemic racism:

- Textbooks are often guilty of blatant sexism and racism. Over the last twenty-four years, total female representation in history and science textbooks has risen from 14 percent to 20 percent, and within that figure, representation of minority women has gone from 2 percent to 6 percent. Improvement, perhaps, but nothing to celebrate.
- Student assessment provides additional evidence of systemic prejudice. Many educators now question the validity of standardized tests, since their environmental and social settings, as well as their specific language, reflect white, middle-class standards. Perhaps this is one of the reasons why blacks and members of other minority groups tend to be highly represented in slow-learner classes and streamed into technical or vocational programs.
- It seems clear that computer programs and materials also reflect white, middle-class standards and values. Many minority families cannot afford the home computers that are becoming a way of life for so many other families. Also, many schools in lower socio-economic areas cannot afford enough computers to give all students adequate hands-on time.
- Minority teachers are not represented proportionally in our classrooms, so minority children do not have access to relevant role models. In one of the biggest

school boards in Canada, for instance, 28 percent of students were born outside the country, but ethnic teachers comprise only 4.5 percent.

What can we do?

Above all, we need to realize that the problem of racism exists everywhere.

School board policies and practices

The human rights paper I referred to suggests the following as part of an effective institutional policy for combatting racism. Perhaps each school board should adopt these specific initiatives.

• Realize the need. Be aware of systemic practices and decide how bad the situation is in your school or your district. Look for bias everywhere.

• Set up a committee to provide clear objectives for affirmative action programs.

• Issue a statement of intent to all those affected. Become committed to the success of the initiatives, while reassuring those who become personally concerned.

• Have the committee draft a plan, revise, if necessary, and set up the implementation.

• Build in monitoring and assessment procedures. Make provision for the arbitration of disputes.

The Victoria County policy includes these intervention strategies:

• Oral communication: School personnel witnessing or being informed of a racial incident are to speak to the perpetrator(s) in order that the student(s) understand the behavior and correct it.

- Oral communication and documentation: More serious offences will involve the principal and/or vice-principal, and the incident will be written up and filed. The student must agree to correct the behavior. In-school counseling may result; suspension is possible; parents or guardians may be contacted and an interview set up.
- Assistance from board personnel: For serious or repeated offences, help may be requested from the system and/or communication personnel. Parents or guardians may be called to assist; suspension of student(s) may occur.
- Expulsion.

The document also lists guidelines for dealing with evidence of racism among the staff, from failing to intervene in a school racial situation to making derogatory statements, treating students in a discriminatory way, or using derogatory material.

I know of one major metropolitan school board that held a ten-day session for teachers to study curricula and take a close look at systemic prejudice in their schools — including the board's hiring practices.

Personal policies and practices

But we cannot let school board policies alone (or the lack of them) dictate our own actions. We are responsible for what goes on within our own classrooms or offices.

John Allan and Judith Nairne, faculty of education instructors at a major university, documented a case study of racial prejudice against a grade five student by some of her classmates. What follows is a summary of their strategies for eliminating the discrimination.

They worked with the whole class, dealing with six topics over a period of five weeks. Their purpose was to strengthen self-esteem and change student attitudes by first placing a positive value on the ethnic identity of *all students*, and then shifting to the understanding and acceptance of other groups. The topics were cumulative: being a new immigrant; being new; being different; being racially different; being respectful; being an original inhabitant. Each lesson began with an introduction and a warm-up. It then systematically explored the students' thoughts and feelings and options for action.

Evaluation followed immediately after the last session, again three months later, and a third time one year later. The results were positive in that they showed a marked improvement in attitudes. Also, no further incidents of prejudice occurred in that classroom.

Abstract teaching about prejudice and racism does not work. Merely teaching about children who live in other lands does not lessen racism. Without deliberate intervention, people continue to accept most readily those who are most like themselves.

As I was writing this last section in my school library, my vice-principal stopped by to tell me about an unfortunate incident. The Jamaican boy I mentioned before, an excellent soccer player, had been playing with some classmates. One of his clever moves had angered someone on the opposite team, who had called him a "#•/! nigger." Children can be cruel. Low self-esteem children are often the worst — they need to put others down so they can feel superior.

I found a simple but effective and illuminating exercise for use in any class, but especially in classes where ethnic children receive some kind of harassment. It suggests that we invite our students to look at a friend and describe their feelings: Why is this person a good friend? What is this person like? What positive qualities does this person have? Next, invite them to view their friend through a piece of colored cellophane and ask themselves: How has this person changed? Are my feelings about this person changed? Does this person's color really make a difference?

Racism is a slippery school problem. When evidence of personal prejudice surfaces, however slight and isolated it may appear, we have to suspect that there is more of it in the school than we think, whether personal, "nice-person," or systemic. We need to be aware of it and fight it on all fronts.

Racism

COPING WITH DISCRIMINATION, Gabrielle Edwards, Rosen Group, 1986. (grades 7-12)

HUMAN RIGHTS IN CANADA: FOCUS ON RACISM, Daniel G. Hill & Marvin Schiff, University of Ottawa, 1988.

POSITIVELY DIFFERENT: CREATING A BIAS-FREE ENVIRONMENT FOR YOUNG CHILDREN, Ana Matiella, Netword Publications, 1991.

START UP MULTICULTURALISM: INTEGRATE THE CANADIAN CULTURAL REALITY INTO YOUR CLASSROOM, Cindy Bailey, Pembroke, 1991.

SEXISM

*Two junior kindergarten boys head off for free play
with their GI Joe book. A little girl follows.*
"You can't play. It's a boy's game."
"Why?"
"Because it's a war game — GI Joe."
"Can't girls play war games?" [Me, observing.]
*"Not this game. There's more badder enemies than
gooder enemies."*
The girl watches, becomes a cat on all fours, meowing.
*"Stop, we can't think! You go in that room while we
work."*
*She goes to a nearby area but continues to peer over the
divider, making cat noises.*
*"Just stay down while we work. What's the matter?
Food?"*
*She nods and one of the boys takes a toy plate, drops it
to the floor and returns to his friend. The two build a block
barrier around themselves.*
*Message? Important male work to be done here. Girls
can get attention by being bothersome and submissive, but
they aren't to be included in the "work."*

• • • • •

A number of years ago I bought a building lot for a summer cottage, the first one to buy into a planned larger development of cottages. Some time later the man who sold me this lot commented: "Of all the people who would buy a lot, you were the least likely in my estimation. And to be the first to build — well, that really surprised me." He meant: "You being a woman and all." It's not easy being a lone woman building or buying a home. Sometimes I used to shake with frustration after a meeting with my builder. And when it comes to financing, the (male) bank manager's first question was: "Who will co-sign?"

For a long time I have considered myself a conscientious practitioner of equal opportunity. I have lined boys and girls up together. I have asked girls to fetch and carry and look after the audio-visual equipment as often as boys. I have encouraged girls to be assertive and strong. I have encouraged boys to let their feelings show. My son has always done his own laundry, and my daughters have no problem changing tires and fuses. My life has been a clear demonstration of how a modern woman juggles home and profession. I have done my best to kill any sexist tendencies in my home and in my school. But as my research progressed, I began to realize how far from non-sexist our society is, how much still needs to be done.

How children think and behave

I asked a discussion circle of junior kindergarten children if they liked being what they were, boy or girl, or if they would change sexes if they could. Two girls said they would change, but they weren't sure why. The boys were unanimous: of course they wanted to stay male. When I asked them why they didn't want to be girls, the replies all implied in some degree that "girls are goofy."

I asked the same questions in a grade three classroom. Here are a few typical comments:

Boys

"I like being a boy because girls have dumb toys." "Boys don't have to have babies." "Because boys are strong." "They get to go fishing." "I like playing with GI toys." "Girls brag about their hair." "Girls are mean."

Girls

"I like being a girl because you get to go shopping." "Boys have to take out the garbage." "We can ride horses." "I get to wear dresses and have long hair." "Girls are pretty. Boys are rude and stupid." "Boys don't let girls do stuff."

I asked the same questions of students in a grade seven class as well, expecting a far greater awareness of sexism, but their comments were almost identical. Both genders saw boys as doing exciting things and girls as going shopping and being pretty. And I had taught these students! They had heard me expound on sexism, on the need for girls to have careers, and on the possibility of single parenting for both sexes. I had told them, for instance, that:

- half of all marriages now end in divorce
- most women outlive their husbands — a young woman today can expect to live until she's eighty
- older women form the largest poverty group
- the number of single fathers is relatively small, but growing

- although some husbands believe they are helping out equally, the working wife does three times as much housework and child care
- more than half of the students at medical school and law school are now female
- the traditional family — mom who stays home, dad who works, children — accounts for something like only 4 to 6 percent of families today
- most women work outside the home and will do so for most of their lives

I later asked both the grade three and grade seven students two more questions.

What do you see yourself doing as an adult?

Grade three

The girls saw themselves primarily as mothers and teachers, with one each as a singer, bank teller, hair dresser, model, and (hurray!) dentist. The boys listed doctor, teacher, hockey player, policeman, firefighter, and computer specialist, or a career in the military. None of them mentioned being a father.

Grade seven

Again, the girls saw themselves mainly as mothers and teachers. One thought she would raise horses, while others suggested interior decorator, nurse, secretary, and lawyer. The boys listed hockey player, forest ranger, pilot, transport driver, president of a company, commander of a SWAT team, carpenter, architect, nuclear physicist, fish and game warden, and cartoonist.

I have since learned that these findings mirror other, more formal studies. Girls are predominantly preoccupied with marriage and motherhood, and assume that a husband will provide for the family, while boys think about a career and "doing things." I should mention also that most of the girls opted for low-paying, non-growth jobs, while the boys dreamed of high-paying, promotion-filled careers. The girls tended to list interests I would call *passive*, while the boys chose *active* hobbies and sports.

What do you feel is most difficult about being your sex?

Grade three

The boys said: "We get in trouble." "We have to work." "Girls are spoiled." The girls said: "We have to do housework." "Boys get to make awesome forts that we can't make." "Boys always tease us." "Boys get to go fishing." "Boys get their way." "We have to have babies."

Grade seven

The males said: "Girls get all the great fashions." "Somehow you don't show your feelings." "You're expected to do things girls can't." "We're given too many responsibilities. Everyone depends on us." "We always get blamed when it's the girls' fault." "Jobs expect more of males." Still, one in four volunteered that it was not hard to be male. Most of the girls, on the other hand, said that it was hard to be female because of periods and getting pregnant. They added: "Guys think they're so good, but they treat girls badly." "Employers hire males before females." "Girls have to be more polite." "We have to do house chores." "Everyone expects girls to be feminine."

What is going on here? Why are the views of these students not undergoing a marked change? They have working mothers. They see their fathers changing the baby, washing dishes. They come from single parent families. Why is the old sexism still there in our children?

Collette Dowling, in her book *The Cinderella Complex*, explains it best. What she basically says is that *gender expectations start early and strong*. From birth, little girls are treated as if they are more fragile. Even as tiny babies they are handled less frequently and less vigorously than boys. One study showed that a girl infant crying was seen by parents as showing fear, a boy as showing anger.

The process of making boys independent begins by age two. During the next several years they are discouraged from any form of "sissy-like" behavior. They receive positive reinforcement for early exploratory ventures and are encouraged to display initiative and rely on themselves instead of others. Girls are over-protected, over-helped, taught that all they have to do to keep help coming is be good — which translates into being timid, cautious, pretty, charming, and polite. Whereas most boys have become fairly independent before they turn six, girls often maintain passivity and dependency into adulthood. Dowling says: "The girl who is passive in the first three years can be counted on to remain passive in early adolescence; by the same token the girl who is passive in adolescence can be expected to be excessively dependent on her parents when she reaches adulthood."

A mother who teaches her daughter to be fearful and avoid risks is starting the child off on a pattern of low self-esteem. These are the girls who will be highly suggestible, who will be easily swayed, and who will set lower standards for themselves than boys. In general, more women in our culture have low self-esteem than men do.

"Not me," you women are saying. "Not my daughters. Not the girls I teach." Yes, you . . . and them . . . and me.

Like Dowling, way down deep I long for someone to look after me and make everything all right. One of my daughters and her boyfriend recently went out in my rowboat. He rowed while she lay back, looking like Cleopatra on the barge. When they came back I asked her why she had not had a turn. "Oh, he liked doing it," she responded. Had she even considered whether she might like doing it? My other daughter made all the arrangements for her wedding, since her fiance lived far away, but if he had lived closer I know she would have asked him to take over. We take it for granted that my son, not any of my daughters, will man the barbecue. (Even our language reinforces it!)

Sexism in schools

I do not think much has changed since the early days of discovering that all is not well between the genders. Boys still build awesome forts and row females across a bay, while girls are busy developing dependency. Boys meet life's challenges; girls are being protected from life's frustrations. One study of classroom interaction at the preschool level showed that teachers give boys more attention, praise them more often, are twice as likely to have extended conversations with them, twice as likely to provide detailed instructions for them to do something, and far more likely to assist little girls by doing things for them.

Another study showed that boys who call out in class receive our attention, while girls who call out are told to raise their hands. The teachers in the three-year study were certain they called on the girls as often as the boys, but the results showed that boys clearly dominated the classroom. They out-talked the girls by a ratio of three to one. Even teachers who were active in equality issues were surprised to see who was talking and who was watching when they examined their own videotaped classroom discussions. In all areas tested — math, science, reading, language arts — the boys participated more, and their participation increased as the school year went on. In fact, the boys called out answers eight times more often than the girls.

The conclusion that systemic sexism exists in schools is not new. In fact, the problem has been discussed for many years in both Canada and the United States. For instance, the 1975 Ontario document, *The Formative Years*, noted that sex roles are largely the result of societal conditioning and stated that "attitudes and socialization practices must change." The authors commented that sex role stereotyping existed in educational materials and classroom practices.

Well after that earlier document, after the Canadian Charter of Rights and Freedoms was passed, after the establishment of an Ontario Advisory Council on Women's Issues, after equity legislation, affirmative action, and media attention, little had changed when, in 1987, the Federation of Women Teachers of Ontario (FWTO) produced a study called *The More Things Change . . . The More They Stay the Same*. It concluded that sexism and racism were still easy to spot in a wide range of classroom materials. Misogyny was thinly veiled and manhood celebrated. Girls and women heroes were absent, as were the wishes and accomplishments of females. "We discovered that while formats, illustrations and some stories had changed, the old metaphor of a world created and controlled by men is still the foundation for most stories." They had a hard time finding women of substance in any of the materials; instead they found "a male world of considerable significance and a female world of little importance."

Schools everywhere are beginning to place less emphasis on specially prepared school readers and more on the use of real children's books, but the same questions must be asked of them. For instance, the author of one study claimed that fairy tales cripple girls because they teach them to be passive and keep their place, in the certain knowledge that someone will come along and rescue them. (An exception is *The Paper Bag Princess* by Robert Munsch.) The question is, would the sustained use of non-sexist books and other learning materials change attitudes? Perhaps. One study that measured prolonged balanced exposure in kindergarten reported that girls were later able to name many more types of jobs available to women. Boys and girls in grades three and four increased their belief that both sexes could succeed in doing what had previously been judged as male work only.

You might try to raise awareness during career week by asking your students to make a list of all the jobs available for males and for females — and hope that one or more perceptive students will raise a puzzled head and ask, "But can't everybody do these?" Indeed! And you could support that notion by inviting a male nurse and a female pilot to visit your class.

Unfortunately, the systemic sexism that pervades curricula throughout North America, with the possible exception of the language arts, makes our task a formidable one, as the following details show.

Mathematics

Every time I hear of a high school graduate — male or female — going into a field that requires math and science, I rejoice. In fact, more and more fields do require those subjects. On the door of our library seminar room hangs a poster listing eighty jobs that are unavailable without high school math. Happily, the number of girls taking math and science courses is growing, although many schools are still having to cope with the fact that girls in general appear to dislike math.

I wanted to know for myself where that dislike originated, so I questioned students in grades two, three, four, seven, and eight.

- In grade two, 23 percent of girls "loved" math, 17 percent "liked" it — together only 40 percent.
- Grade three produced comparable figures.
- In grade four, the combined figures dropped to 28 percent.
- In grades seven and eight only 3 percent "loved" math, but 30 percent "liked" it, depending on what math topic or operation they were covering.
- In the meantime, through all grades about 30 percent of the boys consistently stated that they "loved" math.

By the end of high school approximately two girls in three have dropped math and science from their curriculum altogether. That trend continues in life beyond school as well. About 60 percent of women hold clerical service jobs: low paid, with little advancement, always in danger of obsolescence. Those with mathematical training have not only higher salaries and job security, but also the promise of a secure position as new job fields emerge.

A grade five girl told me she hated math because she did not understand it, and because she had trouble with times tables and with multiplication and division. I asked Jack Thompson, a former math consultant and writer for a math textbook series, why girls develop this kind of negativity toward the subject he loves so much. He ventured that primary teachers "let girls off the hook." He mentioned that boys take more risks and participate far more in any math class, and therefore teacher time is focused on them. Moreover, too much emphasis is still put on the correct answer and not enough on the process, an emphasis sure to produce anxiety in girls whose self-esteem is based more on the need to be "right."

I learned that Jack uses calculators when he teaches. So I arranged for that grade five girl to use one, too, as well as times-tables charts. Why raise anxiety for no good reason? She will use a calculator all her life.

Computer science

Math comfort and discomfort spills over into computer classes. Almost invariably a boy will be called on to help another student with a computer problem, although a girl may be recognized as just as knowledgeable. Even the other girls are likely to ask a boy for help. In introductory computer classes in high school, the ratio of boys to girls is two to one. The bias against females in software and computer advertising is glaringly obvious.

Science

The percentages differ, but the problem remains. Females comprise some 10 percent of higher level physics students. Four graduate physics students at one university I checked were female (out of seventy-two), and in 1986 I found only one woman in Canada who was a full-time professor of physics.

Sports

The following findings from a research report about sexual inequality in school sports programming and participation is almost a decade out of date, but the current situation is much the same.

- Few female role-models were evident in a system controlled by and identified with boys and men at all levels.
- When physical education was optional, female enrollment dropped 5 to 15 percent below that of males.
- More girls than boys participated in intermediate coed *intramural* sports, except gymnastics.
- More boys participated in *interschool* coed athletics.
- In sex-segregated sports, boys played twenty different sports, a total of 131 games. The figures for girls were fifteen and seventy-eight.

When a group of female university students in a phys-ed class were asked if they preferred a male or female coach, they overwhelmingly said male "because they know more."

A male teacher in my school who runs the grade three gym program told me that he believes in coeducational sports, but that he has to separate the class into boys and girls when doing any skill games. Invariably, in mixed company, the girls hold back and let the boys take over. Have a look at how many boys in your school are active with balls at recess. What are the girls doing at the same time?

One suggestion is that prevailing standards of heterosexual attractiveness are not compatible with strong, aggressive sports. Many girls don't participate in high school sports because they do not want to reveal their bodies to the extent that gym shorts and tops force them to. But that simply means that our standards for female attractiveness are unrealistic. There, too, our culture's early carelessness shows up. We are quick to tell little girls that they are pretty and good, but how many times do we tell little boys that they look nice and we like their outfit? What happens to the minds and feelings of little girls who get their strokes for looking pretty?

I read a lot of journals from teenage girls. They write about their appearance, about fights with friends, and about boys, boys, boys. We could all trade stories of bright, achieving girls who choose to "go with" troubled, low-achieving, macho guys. Moms still want their daughters to be popular. The media and advertising promote litheness and perfection of face and body.

I asked one grade eight class, sixteen boys and eighteen girls, to assess their bodies, beginning with the tops of their heads and moving down, listing the body parts they liked in one column, those they disliked in another. Together the boys listed fifty things they did not like about themselves, things like hair, teeth, ears, face, hands, stomach, weight and height. The girls listed 103! They named all the places the boys named plus parts of themselves that just astonished me: ankles, skin color, eyelashes, knuckles, toenails, cheeks, and many more. I asked them where their "standards" came from, and during the discussion the point was made that the women seen on TV and in ads use all kinds of "artificial means" to make themselves look the way they do.

But as I preach to them about accepting themselves, I know I do not make much impact. One grade eight girl confided to me that she was beginning to throw up after eating and could I help, but please do not tell her parents. I had a long talk with her about the dangers of bulimia, and she agreed to take a letter home with some diet suggestions. My daughter is an aerobics instructor who often comments on her "thunder thighs" and the awfulness of her cellulite. Like so many of my students now, she used to go to school without eating breakfast and did not eat anything for lunch either. Except, of course, she would ingest endless colas and munch on sugar sweets.

A note came to my principal's office from a grade three girl: "Dear Mr. B.: Will you get someone to start a secret club just for me and my friends because I want to be skinny and I want to be someone. Please. From A. P.S. Come to my class." Bill handed the note to me. *I want to be someone.* Low self-esteem girls need/want/dream of a boy who will make them "someone." These girls easily become victims, as the chapters on physical and sexual abuse show.

What can we do?

We must do everything we can to balance the inequalities so that both sexes can become more whole human beings. Here is a list of suggestions (incomplete and personal) that I created in response to what I saw going on around me.

- Line boys and girls up randomly, never in two lines based on gender.
- Mix the genders in group work and in classroom seating arrangements.
- Ask girls to fetch, carry, do audio-visual tasks, load computers, etc., as often as you ask boys. Make sure girls get equal access to computers.
- Encourage boys to show their feelings; allow sadness and tears.
- Encourage non-sexist play in the classroom and on the playground.
- Do not reward girls for looking pretty or being quiet, tidy, and well behaved any more often than you reward boys for those same things.
- Focus on all manner of careers for both boys and girls and stress the openness of opportunity for both.
- Bring up achievements of women as often as men.
- Watch for sexist language. Encourage discussions and do surveys to hold sexist views and biases up to the light.
- Make both sexes aware of the bonuses and difficulties of being male or female, or simply human.
- Share your own life with your students. I tell my students about my life struggles and challenges so they see me as a role-model and an example of the changing role of women.

- Take into consideration the existence of single parent families when addressing letters home, planning student-made parent gifts, and arranging parent interviews.
- Watch on the playground and in your classroom for verbal or physical abuse of one sex by the other. Try to instill an appreciation of the hurt that results from being teased about bodies, families, or gender.
- Monitor your interactions with the students. Take special care to call on girls as often as boys.
- Examine all classroom materials critically and, when sexism appears, point out the bias. I try to have a balance of male and female protagonists in any novel study. I watch for exclusionary language and point it out, being especially aware if the material is old. I talk about the unreality of living "happily ever after."
- Watch the library with a critical eye for sexist material as well. If I see a title such as *Track and Field for Boys*, I bring it to the attention of the librarian.
- Watch how you teach math and science. Encourage girls to risk and help them feel good about their efforts. I make these lessons as relaxing and unstressful as I can.
- Watch for inequality in your school's phys ed program and, if you find it, draw it to the attention of other teachers and your administration.
- Do not discipline girls and boys differently.
- Choose both sexes equally for things like awards, special trips and events, or any other recognition.
- Monitor yourself for any personal bias and work to correct it.
- Acknowledge the equal dignity and vulnerability of all your students.

- Teach your students that they always have choices and help them make good ones.
- Make every student responsible for his or her own actions.
- Foster independence and clear thinking in your students and yourself.

Celebrate the positive

I rejoice when male students lament to me that it is hard sometimes to shoulder the burden of all of the effort and "work" of running things, or when they tell me they want to be freer to express their feelings. The impression I get from these young boys is that sometimes being macho hurts. Sometimes they would like to sit back and let a female row the boat across the bay. I teach with men who have no desire for a position of added authority and who are content to be in the ranks. Nurturing comes easily and naturally for many men.

While I was searching for an effective ending for this chapter, I found myself overseeing four grade seven students working together in the library, three girls and one boy. I perked up my ears as I heard one girl say, "I don't know how to do my own laundry and I don't want to learn." The boy replied, with some spirit, "Hey, it's easy. You should learn. I do it all the time." She said no, she did not want to. Another girl, a typically quiet one in most instances, calmly stated, "I'm going to train my husband to do all the wash." I grinned and bent my head to my task.

Sexism

Resources for Adults

BOYS WILL BE BOYS: BREAKING THE LINK BETWEEN MASCULINITY AND VIOLENCE, Myriam Miedzian, Doubleday, 1991.

THE CINDERELLA COMPLEX: WOMEN'S HIDDEN FEAR OF INDEPENDENCE, Colette Dowling, Pocketbook, 1990.

WE'VE ALL GOT SCARS: WHAT BOYS AND GIRLS LEARN IN ELEMENTARY SCHOOL, Raphaela Best, Indiana University Press, 1991.

Resources for Children

COPING WITH SEXISM, Rhonda McFarland, Rosen Group, 1990. (grades 7-12)

THE PAPERBAG PRINCESS, Robert Munsch, Annick Press, 1980.

SEXUALITY

She had undergone an abortion as a 13-year-old, the result of her "curiosity." Four years later she came back to show her beautiful new infant daughter. It wasn't easy to be enthusiastic.

• • • • •

Two grade seven students were caught in a compromising situation in one of the back stairwells. They had used their washroom passes at a prearranged time so they could meet.

• • • • •

At age ten her menstrual periods are so heavy she sometimes has accidents at school. I have sanitary pads in my office, but I'm not always there, and the only other person who has them available is a secretary within earshot of the two male administrators.

• • • • •

Problems of sexuality start early in our schools. The most common problem adolescent and pre-adolescent girls bring to me is, "He's pressuring me to go all the way. What shall I do?" We talk at length, or I counsel at length, through journal entries, about ways of resisting this pressure. When they stop coming or writing, I know they have become sexually active.

One day I heard a local psychiatrist address a large group of high school students on teenage stress. He asked how many students had been in sex education classes. Almost all put up their hands, since the school insists that everyone take phys-ed, and that includes a three-week segment on "health." Then he asked if any teacher had ever discussed with them their worries, fears, sensitivities, and pressures around sex. No hands went up. In my own workshop that same day, I asked nearly 200 students to recall their elementary school experiences. About two-thirds indicated they'd had some sex education classes before high school, but none could remember discussions about their feelings.

I have been teaching the topic to grades five to eight for seventeen years. Traditionally, we have covered puberty and the making of babies, with limited information about birth control and sexually transmitted diseases (STDs). That may seem fairly limited now, but I still remember when the books *Where Did I Come From?* and *What's Happening to Me?* had to be removed from our library shelf because of parental objections. I feel fortunate that our school has purchased the excellent videos based on these two books, and all students in grade five and up watch and enjoy them as part of their sex education classes. There are other changes as well. For instance, the threat of AIDS has forced sex education to be more explicit than it used to be, especially in the use of condoms.

My own experiences make me feel strongly that not every teacher should provide sex education, however. It remains a value-laden topic, particularly on the subjects of homosexuality, masturbation, and abortion.

Our body language and tone of voice may convey attitudes that conflict with our words. Sometimes it is hard for teachers with strong views of their own to be respectful enough of other views. I believe that teachers of this topic should be carefully chosen.

Ideally, of course, sex education should be left to parents. Noted sex educator Sue Johanson advocates that approach, even though many parents and children are uncomfortable discussing the topic. She says: "Straight, honest, non-judgmental talk is what our kids need. They also need to hear about feelings and values. Parents, and schools, are the best people to impart this information." Here is a sample opener: "I'm as nervous and uncomfortable about this discussion as you are, but please hear me out. I'm scared that you'll get AIDS, gonorrhea, chlamydia, or another sexually transmitted disease. I want to be a grandparent some day, you know!" Johanson also suggests that schools can support home discussions, for instance by inviting in an HIV positive guest speaker. Hearing that many people contract AIDS during adolescence from an HIV positive person has a convincing impact on most adolescents.

I researched whether the parents of the students in my own grade five and grade seven classes had discussed sex with them. Here are the results (answers remained anonymous).

Grade five
Thirteen boys indicated that they had not talked with their parents about the subject at all; nine moms and two dads had initiated conversations separately, or answered questions. Seven girls reported no discussion; seven moms and two dads had engaged in

one-on-one conversation, and one girl reported a discussion with both parents.

Grade seven

Eight boys had discussed sex with moms alone, seven with moms and dads together, and three alone with dads; seven had had no conversation. Four girls had had no talks; nineteen moms initiated a discussion separately, and three moms and dads spoke together with their daughters.

Almost half of the younger children had received no information, a figure reduced to one-quarter two years later. At face value that is not too bad, although it may be that the "talk" was as limited as the parents simply saying, "Don't get pregnant" or, "Here's the way to avoid getting a girl pregnant." There is so much for children to hear and absorb that they need to hear key information over and over again.

It seems inevitable that schools will have to spend time and effort on sex education — particularly about AIDS — for a long time to come, so we had better be prepared for it. In the United States, *HIV-AIDS Instructional Guide* for grades K through 12, published by the New York State Board of Education, is used as a model throughout the country and promoted by the National Center for Disease Control.

For Canadian teachers I can highly recommend an excellent, comprehensive guide called *AIDS: Preparing Your School and Community*, produced by the Canadian Association of Principals. One of its many valuable checklists helps teachers review their own suitability for taking on this topic. With permission, I include it here for your guidance. It suggests that you will likely feel comfortable teaching sex education if you:

- believe it is a much needed curriculum offering
- are enthusiastic about teaching it
- believe that sexual adjustment is an important aspect of overall adjustment and personality
- are comfortable with your own sexuality and the topics to be covered
- are clear about your personal code of ethics and values
- are open-minded and non-judgmental with respect to values, attitudes, beliefs, and behavior that may differ from your own
- are respectful of different cultural and religious values and beliefs
- are committed to the rights of parents as primary sex educators of their children
- are able to relate to students effectively, with honesty, warmth, and sensitivity
- are willing to learn and are excited rather than threatened by the prospect of new information and teaching methodologies
- are respected by students, parents, administrators, and fellow teachers
- have a sense of humor

As part of my teaching workshops on sexuality, I give participants a set of fifty questions, drafted anonymously by grades seven and eight students, and ask the teachers to evaluate their own comfort level in answering each question on the list.

The question the majority of them find most difficult to answer is: "How do I know if I am homosexual?" The issue of homosexuality is important to face since, according to Sue Johanson, 1 in 10 of our kids are homosexual and most boys have same-sex fantasies and are firmly convinced they must be gay.

Some communities prefer to avoid the issue of AIDS altogether: "It will never happen here." However, my own ministry of education is very direct in its resource document about AIDS education: "A mandatory unit of study on AIDS shall be part of the health education program in grade seven or eight. The mandatory unit on AIDS forms part of the total health education program under the category related to human sexuality. The aim is to help students develop and maintain a positive and reasonable attitude towards their sexuality and, within that context, to act on their knowledge and to make positive decisions about matters affecting their health."

I consider these wise words. No matter where we teach or what the current policies of our school district are, we are called on to care about the safety and happiness of our students. And that care can find expression in the stress we put on the safest means of birth control and of preventing STDs: the words and actions that say "No!"

Unfortunately, too few of our students take that advice to heart. A 1988 study (again Canadian) on youth and AIDS found that 31 percent of grade nine males and 21 percent of females had experienced intercourse at least once, as had nearly 33 percent of all grade eleven students and 75 percent of all those in first year university. Only 15 percent of grade eleven and 13 percent of college/university students stated that a fear of AIDS would prevent them from having sex. Nor do sexually active young adults like to use condoms. In

Canada, approximately one in four never use them; in the United States, the number is one in three.

In a recent survey, adolescents were asked their beliefs about pregnancy. Many think that you can't get pregnant if

- you have sex only once in a while
- have sex with your eyes open
- won't get pregnant if he doesn't ejaculate
- the woman doesn't have an orgasm
- you have sex standing up
- it's the first time
- you don't take your clothes off
- the girl takes an aspirin and a Coke before intercourse
- you crush up a birth control pill and give it to the boy before intercourse
- the girl douches with Coke, Pepsi, vinegar, Dettol, etc.
- the boy uses Saran Wrap or a balloon as a condom
- she eats contraceptive jelly

Where were the parents of these children when they needed correct information? Where were the schools?

In another illuminating study, Planned Parenthood found that the overwhelming reason teens give for agreeing to sex is peer pressure. Next come curiosity, "everyone is doing it," love, and sexual gratification.

Several years ago at a conference on sexuality, I learned that 1 million teenagers in Canada were sexually active, and that 30 to 50 percent of them often used no birth control. I heard Sue Johanson say in 1988 that one out of ten high school girls becomes pregnant. Only a few years ago, 85 percent of teenage mothers gave their babies up for adoption; today 90 percent keep them. Lots of babies are having lots of babies.

What can we do?

When we look at these statistics and misconceptions, it is clear that we need to consider more than the mechanics of birth control. We also need to pay attention to the psychological factors. Who are the needy children? Who are the leaders and what is the basis of their leadership? Which ones have a low self-esteem or poor decision-making skills? Which ones are already setting themselves up to be victims in life? Which ones are the passive followers? And how can we help these children?

Most of what we need to do focuses on communication and awareness. We need to read the results of those surveys to our children. We need to talk about how life is changed forever by a pregnancy, both for the girl and for the boy, who may have to pay support for twenty years. We need to teach strategies for decision-making, perhaps by role-playing saying "no" and meaning it. As difficult as it may seem, we must try to combat the whole fantasy notion of romance. (Notice how much of what I've just said concerns the *feeling* part of sexuality.)

In my school, we begin teaching about sex in grade five. We first send a letter home informing the parents, so they can use the time beforehand to have any talks they may have been putting off. We use the video and book *Where Did I Come From?* and several other books you will find listed in the references. We tell the girls where to obtain sanitary napkins and tampons, how to dispose of them in school, and invite a general sharing of their knowledge about menstruation. They also need to know what is involved in getting help with birth control. Many are scared that a pelvic exam will be painful, or that the doctor will discuss the visit with parents.

In grade six, we review and then use the book and video *What's Happening to Me?*, giving the students opportunities to ask questions anonymously. A special class is held for the girls on menstruation; I also talk to the boys separately about what the girls will be experiencing.

In grades seven and eight, we first review earlier topics and then begin the AIDS unit, where we also cover other STDs and birth control — plus anything else they ask about, which is likely to be everything. Before the grade eight students graduate, we have "the talk" together. This is the time when I say to them: "It's up to you to decide not to have sex until it is the right time for you."

The most common question I am asked by intermediate students is "When will I be ready for sex?" I always reply, "When you are thirty-five." After all the exclamations and hoots of derision, I go on: "Now that I have your attention, my answer is this: the longer you wait, the better it will be for you. Sex in the back seat of a car is always disappointing for the girl and often for the boy, too. Eighty-six percent of sexual activity takes place in the boy's home. Most pregnancies begin in the rec room of the house when the parents are upstairs. How can that be satisfying?"

I do all that I can to urge a "no" mentality, but I know my students are experimenting. So I tell them how to obtain birth control, and we always discuss abortion. Now that the spectre of AIDS is very real, sexual experimentation can be extremely dangerous.

Can this type of program work? Can we actually lower the number of kids who are sexually active? A high school phys ed teacher confessed to me recently that he is becoming totally overwhelmed by his lack of success. My question to him was: "How can you be sure you're having no success?" All we hear about are the dramatic failures, not the private decisions to opt for celibacy or safe sex.

Unfortunately, a more pronounced effectiveness may take more time and effort than we are able to give. The guide for principals that I mentioned earlier maintains that school health programs cannot produce significant changes, either in health behaviors or in knowledge and attitudes, without some *forty to fifty hours of instruction*. That means ten hours per year between grades seven and twelve. In the meantime, one out of every ten babies born in New York City is testing HIV positive. Deaths from AIDS are rising in the young adult and child populations everywhere in the world. Terms like gonorrhea, warts, crabs, herpes, and chlamydia had better become familiar to our students.

Minimum goals for an effective unit on sexuality should include:

• the elimination of myths and misinformation
• an understanding of what constitutes "safe sex"
• explicit information about AIDS and other STDs

- the acquisition of problem-solving and decision-making skills to combat peer pressure
- drug awareness (since AIDS is also spread by needle sharing)
- opportunity to develop communication skills

But we have a long way to go before frank and open discussions of sex become a normal part of school life. To test my students' comfort level, I pass a condom around the class. The boys' faces turn red and the girls squeal and throw it to the next person as if it were a poisonous snake. It is not a great attitude toward a protection device that could save their lives!

We also have to keep in mind that some of our students may have been sexually abused, perhaps still are. If I know them, I quietly invite those students to sit by the door, monitor their reactions, and allow them to leave if the discussion becomes too uncomfortable for them. One girl simply could not attend at all. All the class ever knew was that her parents did not want her to be there.

These are tough issues, and it is tempting to dodge them. But if we want our young people to become healthy, fully functioning sexual beings, sex education must not stress only the fearful aspects of sexuality, the should-nots and the must-nots. It also has to include the message that sex is a lovely, warm, beautiful part of loving and being human. That is a difficult, double-edged lesson children have to learn at a difficult time of life. On the one hand their "happy hormones" are urging them to do what is natural — to mate. On the other hand they are being taught all the horrors of unsafe, unwise sex. As I teach them, I try to be aware of the power I hold to build or to damage. I try to approach sexuality with candor, but also with the reverence that is its due. I try to temper the harsh realities with the glow of intimacy, and how we need that in our lives.

Sexuality

Resources for Adults

AIDS: PREPARING YOUR SCHOOL & COMMUNITY, Canadian Association of Principals, Health & Welfare Canada, 1990.

CM - REVIEW JOURNAL OF CANADIAN MATERIALS FOR YOUNG PEOPLE, Vol. XIX/5 October 1991, Canadian Library Association, "The New Facts of Life: Resources to help teach your students about Aids."

GROWING UP SERIES - A SEX-ED PROGRAM FOR CLASSROOMS [includes 3 VHS cassettes and teachers guide] National Film Board of Canada (see Appendix for more information).

NOW THAT YOU KNOW: WHAT EVERY PARENT SHOULD KNOW ABOUT HOMOSEXUALITY, Betty Fairchild, Harcourt, Brace Jovanovich, 1989.

LETTERS TO JUDY: WHAT YOUR KIDS WISH THEY COULD TELL YOU, Judy Blume, Putnam, 1986.

NATIONAL AIDS CLEARINGHOUSE
Canadian Public Health Association
400-1565 Carling Avenue
Ottawa, Ontario
LK1Z 8R1 (Canada)
(613)725-3769 • FAX (613)725-9826

NATIONAL AIDS INFORMATION CLEARINGHOUSE
P.O. Box 6003
Rockville, MD 20850
1-800-458-5231 (U.S.)

RAISING SEXUALLY HEALTHY CHILDREN, Lynn Leight, Avon, 1988.

SEXUALITY EDUCATION: A RESOURCE BOOK, Carol Cassell and Pamela Wilson, Garland, 1989.

University of Guelph Annual Conference and Training Institute on Sexuality. The conference attracts educators, nurses, physicians, therapists, social workers, clergy and other professionals.

Resources for Children

AIDS Hot-line for Teens (U.S.) 1-800-234-TEEN

BEING BORN, Sheila Kitzinger, Putnam, 1986. (grades 2-5)

THE BARE NAKED BOOK, Heather Collins and Kathy Stinson, Annick, 1986. (ages 3-5)

ONE TEENAGER IN TEN: WRITING BY GAY AND LESBIAN YOUTH, edited by Ann Heron, Alyson Press, 1983. (grades 7-12)

TALK SEX: THE SEX LADY TELLS IT LIKE IT IS, Sue Johanson, Penguin, 1989.

WHERE DID I COME FROM?, Peter Mayle, Lyle Stuart, 1973.

WHAT'S HAPPENING TO ME?, Peter Mayle, Lyle Stuart, 1975.

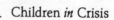

PART IV

SELF-ESTEEM

"Apart from the problems that are biological in origin, I cannot think of a single psychological difficulty — from anxiety and depression, to fear of intimacy or success, to alcohol or drug abuse, to underachievement in school or at work, to spouse battering or child molestation, to sexual dysfunction or emotional immaturity, to suicide or crimes of violence — that is not traceable to poor self-esteem. Of all the judgment calls we pass, none is as important as the one we pass on ourselves. Positive self-esteem is a cardinal requirement of a fulfilling life."

Nathanial Branden

• • • • •

How do you feel about being you? Are you glad to see that face when you get up in the morning? Do you celebrate who you are? If you are like me, you are comfortable with parts of yourself and not so comfortable with others.

One benefit of my own wide reading about self-esteem has been the realization that we are made up of many selves. Children are aware of only a limited number of selves: family member, learner, athlete, friend. Our maturity enables us to recognize more selves: a physical being, a male/female, an emotional and spiritual self, a son/daughter/spouse/sibling/single person/parent, a practical and creative professional, a money manager, an unbiased self, a spontaneous/tolerant, assertive/accepting self . . . the list goes on.

Happily, most of us have many strong areas to fall back on when one or more of our other selves become shaky. In fact, during the period of my greatest personal stress, my still intact professional self was able to support me until I could rebuild the other selves. Changes in life such as gaining weight, becoming handicapped through illness, children leaving home, retiring, or suffering the death of a parent can cause a reshuffling of one's sense of self.

It is easy to understand and accept that the more positive parts of ourselves we can acknowledge, the better we will adjust; the fewer good selves, the more difficult rebuilding becomes.

Self-esteem assaulted

I once spotted the following notice on the door of a primary classroom.

Our classroom covenant
I have the right to be happy and to be treated with kindness in this room. This means that no one will laugh at me, ignore me, or hurt my feelings. I have the right to be myself in this room. This means that no one will treat me unfairly because I am fat or thin, fast or slow, boy or girl.

Please go back and reread that covenant with the word "house" for "room." Were you treated that way in the house you grew up in? The beautiful flower faces in our early photographs capture our young enthusiasm and joy in life. We stand surrounded by caring parents and significant others. And yet I read somewhere that 77 percent of communication between parent and child, husband and wife, teacher and student, employer and employee is negative. Very early in our lives we begin to hear that we are not altogether the beautiful flower the photographs portray. Dark messages rain down on us: "Don't touch," "You're a bad boy/girl," "You're too sloppy/loud/slow/silly."

From my unhappy, critical mother I internalized an encyclopedia of negatives. Achievements over the years have made some of my selves feel okay, but I still find it difficult to accept my total self as an okay being, as a person who is loved for who I am. To others my armor looks strong, my mask solid, but inside hides a very shaky two-year-old. One professional development day, a speaker named Dr. William Purkey reached right into that little child self within me, and much of what follows comes from his talk and from his book, *Inviting School Success*.

In his lovely southern drawl, Purkey used the image of the psychological bucket I touched on earlier. Children who have experienced lots of love, acceptance, and fair discipline have buckets that are filled high. They have a real sense of okay-ness and, when difficulties come their way, they can draw lots of positive affirmation from their buckets.

You can spot full-bucket children easily. Their eyes sparkle with curiosity about the world, they accept you in a loving way, they are polite and agreeable, and their bodies exude life. Whether they are shy or outgoing, they accept who they are because they have been accepted as cherished beings by others. Their sunny dispositions invite more positive strokes from the school and their community at large, and their buckets continue to be topped up.

Contrast these children with those who have been pushed around, ignored, or physically or sexually abused; with children of alcoholics who constantly live with uncertainty and fear; or with children whose separated parents war over them. Contrast them with children who have received uneven experiences of affection at best and, at worst, constant harsh, punitive, discipline. Contrast them with children of over-permissive or over-protective parents. Contrast them with children who are constantly labeled "stupid," "dummy," "can't-you-ever-do-anything-right?"

It is low self-esteem we see when "brats" act up in shopping malls. It is low self-esteeem we see when children are difficult to deal with. Children who lie, steal, hit others (and sometimes us!), mouth back, are messy — these are children who do not like themselves much.

Purkey has this to say about the importance of self-esteem: "The primary purpose of education, as we view it, is to invite people to realize their potential, to meet the needs of society, and to participate in the progress of civilization. There is a significant relationship between self-concept and school achievement. Students' perceptions of themselves as learners serve as personal guidance systems to direct their classroom behavior. Because the self-concept of students as learners is a critical part in their academic performance, a professional understanding of self-concept theory, coupled with skills for interpreting how students view themselves as learners are important tools."

He goes on to list four key self-concept factors that bear on school performance.

Relating

This refers to the level of trust and appreciation students maintain toward others. Students who relate well think in terms of "our school" and "my classmates." They stay calm when things do not go right. They can express negative feelings without losing control. Their opposites refer to "that school" and "those kids." They criticize others to make themselves feel better.

When I teach the self-esteem units that are part of the grades seven and eight guidance programs, I use the analogy of a teeter-totter. People who put others down feel up, but only for a short time, for they are soon put down in turn. I try to help my students change their thinking and find strategies to offset the influence of the people who have to put others down. "I can always count on you for a put-down," or "Why are you trying to make me feel bad?" are phrases found in a filmstrip set I use for fostering positive self-esteem.

Eleanor Roosevelt once said, "No one can make you feel bad without your permission." Dr. Purkey says the same thing this way: "If you're feeling bad, then you're thinking wrong."

Asserting

Students who score high in self-esteem speak up for themselves, feel a sense of control, are not afraid to ask questions, and are active in their own learning. Low scorers stop trying and become discouraged. Like the trained circus animal that will not leave its cage even though the door is open, these children never find it easy to believe they can do much. Lack of assertion produces anxiety — "I have no power" — and anxious students are future failures.

I once taught history to a special group of ten grade eight students who had come to hate and fear the subject because of all the testing they had experienced. At the outset I promised them good marks if they cooperated and kept neat notebooks. I also pledged to test only at the end of the year, and even then we would draft the test together. I tried to create a relaxed tone, focusing on history as the stories of real people. I made learning active — we imagined what it would be like to witness a "Loyalist" being tarred and feathered and made a large mural for our school district history fair. (It won a prize!) When the group discovered that they were overtaking the regular class, they took great delight in comparing notes with the others. In the end, all but one of the students finished the year with satisfactory marks.

Investing

This refers to the creative part of the student as learner, the willingness to risk, to make predictions, and to accept challenges. Children scoring high in self-esteem see reward in the activity itself, in the process, in trying out solutions. Low scorers need the safety of predictability. (And it does not help that we commonly allow only one second for response-to-question time!) Even when we stress that it is through making errors that they learn, children have little tolerance for peer error. It is no wonder that only the strong ones continue to try, when saying or doing something incorrectly is likely to produce sniggers from the rest of the class. Frequently it is the kids with a low sense of self who are the first to jeer or comment. For those whose psychological bucket is permanently low, peer negativity is paralyzing.

Coping

Students with positive self-esteem see themselves as able and willing to cope. They believe in their own academic ability and feel a sense of pride in their achievements. They pay attention, work carefully, finish their work, and expect to succeed. Teachers who have such a group will say they have died and gone to heaven. Low scorers experience great frustration. Fear of failure makes them stop trying — they feel they cannot cope. They know deep inside themselves that they *are* the labels that have been hung on them: stupid, clumsy, ugly. They are filled with fear. Learned helplessness is a tragedy for both student and teacher. Both feel so lost.

What can we do?

Purkey suggests strategies for gently coaxing out of these hurting children some belief in themselves.

- Relating: Use "we" statements frequently, use the children's names, use peer tutoring, and become what he calls "professionally inviting" in all ways. I call it using your warm heart.

- Asserting: Allow, invite, and respect dialogue about differing points of view, and role-play socially acceptable ways of dealing with self-expression.
- Investing: Allow three to five seconds for responses to questions, ask open-ended questions, and ask the same student a related question to help establish an awareness of success.
- Coping: Point out errors tactfully, do not focus on negatives or poor performance, help the children understand not only their mistakes but also that mistakes are normal in learning and living. And, I would add, own up to your own goofs.

Rudolf Dreikers believed that *encouragement* is everything. Discouraged children become behavior problems. Children's behavior is a gauge of their self-acceptance. Children who do not believe in their own worth will not try to be useful and will not contribute or participate. Their behavior will be merely provocative and useless. Bullies are discouraged children who believe they have worth only when they show power. Their victims are children who do not even believe in their own power.

"Active parenting," grounded in the theories of Dreikers and Alfred Adler, teaches that the most important quality parents (and teachers) can give to their children is courage. Courage is fostered by asking for the children's opinion and advice and then by assigning responsibilities they can easily master — and avoiding the temptation to rescue.

Some of the discouraging strategies we commonly use are focusing on negative expectations or mistakes, comparing, expecting perfection, and over-protecting. We send children messages through both words and body language (more easily read by children than we realize) that include ridicule, sarcasm, annoyance, rejection, anger, distrust, discouragement, and impatience. And the children's response is aggression, indifference, failure, withdrawal, tension, hostility, fear, guilt, and submissiveness. Many of our students live in a catch-22 situation. Those who need our praise and positive reactions the most get them the least. Those who need our impatience and negative reactions the least get them most consistently. Our job as educators is to recognize these factors and do all we can not to add to the burdens of these children.

Here is William Purkey again. "Whatever else a school may be, it should not be a place where students are embarrassed, insulted, or humiliated. Demeaning school practices such as public ridicule, invidious comparisons, deliberate humiliation, and corporal punishment must be eliminated if a school is to consider itself personally and professionally inviting."

Dr. Arnold Rincover wrote a column in the *Toronto Star* in 1988 that contains some suggestions that might help to lessen the amount of negative communication we lay on our students. He begins by saying that we should *expect good behavior* and take its existence for granted. Criticism is necessary for growth and learning, but it must be constructive and kind. Here are some of the strategies he suggests.

Be selective.

Pick one thing that is easy to change, so success will follow. Be patient and get to other problems gradually. The child is not likely to feel attacked, since you are dealing with only one small bit of behavior. In other words, do not "kitchen sink" and throw in everything you have wanted to mention or have been harping on for ages — a pattern perhaps more common in families than in classrooms.

Always find something to praise.

Sincere praise will get you there ten times faster than a PhD in nagging. There will always be one thing you can mention positively. (Did you ever wonder what would happen if we gave back a piece of writing with every correct word ticked?)

Don't criticize by saying something is wrong.

Instead, suggest a way to do it better: "Have you thought of . . .?" "What if you tried . . .?" "Would it be better to . . .?"

When the child does it right, give credit.

Let the child know you are really pleased. (But do not overdo it. Kids easily read beneath the words.)

The good news is that self-concept can be changed and that we can be instrumental in effecting changes. The bad news is that it may take a long time to notice any difference in particular children. Sometimes we are trying to make dents in long-held central beliefs, and it may not be easy to shift the children away from their negative self-perceptions. Noticing and complimenting changes are extremely important.

We all want our own children to have warm, supportive teachers, and we want to be warm and supportive ourselves. Of course we are responsible for teaching curriculum content, but more important is teaching the whole child. I have come to believe that much of the effectiveness of our teaching depends on *how* we bring curriculum and children together. It does not matter too much which method we use to teach. What counts is our own enthusiasm and our belief in the children as learners.

It may sound trite, but it is as true in our classrooms as anywhere else: we should treat others as we wish to be treated. The point was brought home to me a year ago during a Lions-Quest "Skills for Adolescence" training session. One of the participants came in late and immediately the instructor stopped talking, looked over at him and began, in a deadly sarcastic voice, to berate him for his rudeness to the rest of us. My insides clenched up and I felt sick — and I was sure the student felt infinitely worse. But the scene had been set up deliberately to give us a firsthand sense of what our children often experience as they look on while their peers "get it." That onlooker experience was agonizing to me as an adult; I shudder to think what the children who receive our wrath or sarcasm must experience. The instructor suggested that we try to imagine ourselves sitting among our students as we teach, and measure the success of our lesson not by how brilliant we were, but by how good the students felt afterwards.

Barbara Coloroso is another person worth hearing or watching on video. She focuses on fair discipline and provides several strategies for increasing self-esteem. She also suggests six critical life messages that we ought to try every day in every way to give to each and every student.

- I believe in you.
- I trust you.
- I know you can handle it.
- You are listened to.
- You are cared for.
- You are very important to me.

The children who have consistently heard these six messages at home usually come to us as eager learners. It is up to us to give them to those who have not heard them at home, in such a way that they are believed and internalized.

A researcher once asked over two thousand adults to think about the teachers they had had as children and tell why they remembered those teachers. It was both the very bad and the very good teachers they recalled. And it was not for the brilliance of their pedagogy that they remembered the good ones, but for the degree of warmth they imparted. I still remember sitting on the knee of my grade one teacher as I read to her, but I remember nothing else about her. I remember how some of us went to meet our grade two teacher every day as she returned to school after lunch, but I remember nothing else about her. And I remember the grade six teacher who one day strapped us for spelling errors. True! One strap for each error. I was a good speller and I got only one. But when she said she was going to do the same with fractions the next day, I was terrified because math was always my worst subject. My dad called the school and complained (it turned out he was not the only parent who did), because when he whistled up the stairs to waken me as usual, I did not come down. He found me huddled in a heap on the landing.

No child should feel such fear about any school or any teacher. Dr. Purkey speaks of teachers who live a "professional half-life." Teachers like that twisted grade six teacher do not have *any* life. How does one forgive such a teacher? Two years ago I flew out to Alberta to a school reunion and she was there, looking old and worn. I could not speak to her. If you are a teacher, how do you want to be remembered by your students? If they meet you in future years at reunions or on the street, will their faces show anticipation and delight? Or will they turn away as I did?

In the end, we always come back to that face in the mirror. To the one person who is always with you and always will be. To the one person you should celebrate and treat well. Purkey recognizes the importance of our own self-esteem. He tells us to stand tall, dress well, eat less, take exercise, become involved, and find ways to be present in the world. He provides tips for us to maintain our personal energy level and nurture ourselves physically, emotionally, and spiritually.

- Take pleasure in stillness. Enjoy silence. Contemplate and meditate on who you are, where you came from, and where you are going. Being at one with yourself can be deeply rewarding.
- Keep in reasonable shape. It is important to maintain the body in which you live.
- Plan a long life. Take personal responsibility for your own life support system. Be choosy about how much and what you eat. Eliminate cigarettes and other injurious substances. Maintain health care and fasten your seat belt.
- Give yourself a celebration. Make a pledge to do

something special for just yourself in the immediate future: a bubble bath, a fishing expedition, a good novel, a shopping trip, a new outfit, a favorite meal, a game of golf, a film or play . . . celebrate!

- Recharge your batteries. Handle short-term burnout by talking things over with a friend you think has good sense. Do not accept a lot of guilt and anxiety.
- Live with a flourish. Find satisfaction from many sources, including hobbies and activities unrelated to your professional life. As much as realistically possible, surround yourself with things you like. Laugh a little. Take a few risks, travel and assert yourself. The goal is to avoid drabness.

Not a bad list, right? I especially want to be able to "live with a flourish."

There is no magic dust to spread over our schools that will help the people who work in them, students and teachers alike, to walk lighter. Each one of us must pledge to try to raise the self-esteem and self-confidence of ourselves and our students — and do it. Where to begin? There are books and workshops available; there are night courses and people to model ourselves after.

It all begins with self-awareness.
It all begins with commitment.
It all begins with us.
We *can* make a difference.

Self-Esteem

Resources for Adults

CANADIAN INSTITUTE FOR CONFLICT RESOLUTION
Provides information, training, advice and guidance on
collaborative conflict resolution to those in education, business,
spiritual council and law.
St. Paul's University
223 Main St.
Ottawa, Ontario
Canada, K1S 1C4
(613)789-2229 • FAX (613)782-3005

CHILDREN: THE CHALLENGE, Rudolf Dreikurs and Vicky Soltz, Dutton,
1991.

CREATIVE CONFLICT RESOLUTION, William J. Kreidler, Scott Foresman,
1984. More than 200 activities for keeping peace in the k-6 classroom.

DISCIPLINE: WINNING AT TEACHING/PARENTING WITHOUT
BEATING YOUR KIDS, Barbara Coloroso, Kids Are Worth It! (Other Kids
Are Worth It! materials listed in Appendix.]

DISCIPLINE: CREATING A POSITIVE SCHOOL CLIMATE, Barbara
Coloroso, Kids Are Worth It! (see above)

HOW TO RAISE YOUR SELF-ESTEEM, Nathanial Branden, Bantam, 1987.

INVITING SCHOOL SUCCESS: A SELF-CONCEPT APPROACH TO
TEACHING AND LEARNING, Dr. William Purkey, Wadsworth
Publishing, 1984.

LIONS QUEST - Canada 1-800-265-2680; U.S. 1-800-288-6401

SMILING AT YOURSELF: EDUCATING YOUR CHILDREN ABOUT
STRESS AND SELF-ESTEEM, Network Publishing, 1991.

Resources for Children

TEEN ESTEEM: A SELF-DIRECTING MANUAL FOR YOUNG ADULTS, Pat
Palmer and Melissa Froehner, Impact Publishing, 1989.

STICK UP FOR YOURSELF! EVERY KID'S GUIDE TO PERSONAL POWER
AND POSITIVE SELF-ESTEEM, Gershen Kaufman and Lev Raphael, Free
Spirit Press, 1990.

AFTERWORD

If the desperate child has one human being who cares, one person who can hear the often non-verbal plea for help, a disaster can often be prevented.

Elizabeth Kubler-Ross

•••••

This was probably not easy material for you to read — it certainly wasn't easy for me to write. And there's so much more! It doesn't even touch on some of the important issues that may surface in critical situations involving the children around you.

Fortunately, many school boards are aware of the overwhelming need and are doing all they can to help their teachers. My own board has a "crisis resource" person and three "behavior resource" teachers on staff, as well as a social worker, to assist us when we have to deal with crisis situations. Unfortunately, those people are often stretched to the limit themselves. So many schools! So many hurting kids! And those extra resources don't lessen our need to cope on a daily basis.

I'm not an expert, just a teacher writing from my own experiences and my own learning — and I still have much more learning to do. But the knowledge I've gained and the strategies I've learned have helped me tremendously in the past months, and I hope this book can help you a little with your own coping. If nothing more, it will perhaps heighten your awareness of the issues and help you use your natural warmth to be more present than you already are in the lives of hurting children.

At a recent workshop on drug education someone said, "If not you, who? If not now, when?" I leave those questions with you.

Appendix

SOURCES

THE CHILDRENS' SMALL PRESS COLLECTION
Fourth Avenue
Ann Arbor, Michigan
U.S.A. 48104
1-800-221-8056
Hard-to-find good books and music for children, parents and family support professionals.

FREE SPIRIT PUBLISHING INC.
400 1st Avenue N. Suite 616
Minneapolis, Minnesota
Excellent collection of books on social and emotional issues for teachers, parents and kids.

HEALTH PROMOTIONS DIRECTORATE
HEALTH SERVICES AND PROMOTION
HEALTH & WELFARE CANADA
2221 Yonge St.
Room 605
Toronto, Ontario M4S 2B4
(416)973-6485
Many materials available. Send for catalog.

KIDS ARE WORTH IT!
P.O. Box 621108
Littleton, Colorado
80162, USA
800 729-1588
FAX: (303)972-1204
Internationallly recognised expert on school discipline and parenting offers audio, video cassettes and teaching guides.

KIDS HELP PHONE - in Canada 1-800-668-6868
For further information on how to promote the Kids Help Phone in
your school or region write or phone:
Kids Help Phone
Jeunesse, J'ecoute
P.O. Box 513, STe. 100
2 Bloor St. West
Toronto, Ontario
M4W 3E2
(416)921-7823

NATIONAL CHILD SAFETY COUNCIL
P.O. Box 1368 Jackson, Michigan
49204-1368 (U.S.)
(517) 764-6070
World's largest and oldest organization dedicated to safety of
children. Full spectrum of programs.

NATIONAL FILM BOARD OF CANADA
150 John Street
Toronto, Ontario M5V 3C3
800-267-7710
Excellent collection of video learning materials.

PARENTBOOKS
201 Harbord St.
Toronto, Ontario
M5S 1H6
(416)537-8334
FAX: (416) 537-9499
Extensive selection of books for parents, teachers and related
professionals.

THAT OTHER BOOKSTORE
745 Queen St. W.
Toronto, Ontarioo M6J 1G1
800-668-2665
FAX: (416)36 0-0531
Self-help and recovery books.

Printed in Canada